To Ralph &

I hope _____, _____ _____

some happy memories.

Hank

One thousand copies
of the first edition of

Rendezvous In the Bush

by

Henry T. Folsom

have been published by
Trophy Room Books

This is copy number....*140*........

Signed by the Author ....

Henry T. Folsom

441

Rendezvous In the Bush

Rendezvous In the Bush

Henry T. Folsom

Trophy Room Books

Rendezvous In the Bush
Copyright © 1999 Henry T. Folsom
Published by Trophy Room Books

Folsom, Henry T.
Rendezvous In the Bush

Library of Congress Catalog Card Number: 99-60145
ISBN 1-882458-21-4

c 1999 Agoura CA
First Edition

Readers wishing to receive the Trophy Room Books catalogs featuring many fine books on travel and adventure in Africa, Arabia, Asia and North America should write to:

Trophy Room Books
Box 3041
Agoura CA 91301 USA
Telephone 818 889-2469   FAX 818 889-4849
Internet: www.trophyroombooks.com

Printed in the United States of America

Trophy Room Books
Publishers and Booksellers

Dedication

To the memory of my dear wife, Phyllis P. Folsom ("Peeko"), who was my partner in marriage for over 45 happy years, who gave me three wonderful children, and who endured four safaris into the African bush — largely without complaint — I dedicate this collection of memories.

And to the memory of my father, H. Lloyd Folsom, who throughout my childhood enthralled me with tales of his African hunting, who introduced me to the joys of the woods, the mountains, and the wild creatures that live in them. To the memory of him with whom I shared many campfires, but who did not live to hear the tales of *my* African adventures; to the memory of him who taught me to love the wilderness and the animals I hunted, I also dedicate this journey into nostalgia.

Contents

Acknowledgements

Over the several years it has taken to compile these reminiscences I have availed myself of help from a number of people, and I owe all of them my sincere gratitude:

To David Ommanney, my professional hunter on five safaris, for writing the foreword to this book.

To Russell B. Aitken, an old friend at the Camp Fire Club and an African hunter *par excellence*, whose use of the epitaph of Ashurbanipal in his book, *Great Game Animals of the World*, led me to close a chapter with a slightly different translation of it.

To Freeman Keith, a retired printer, for his very thorough proofreading of my manuscript.

To my son, Henry, for several of the photographs.

To Tamara ("Tami") Miglio, who accompanied Phyllis and me on safari in 1987 and 1990, also for several of the photographs.

To my late sister, Charlotte Saunders, for sending me our father's article on lion hunting, which has been incorporated into my text.

To my late wife, Phyllis, who offered helpful advice throughout most of the writing of this manuscript, and even wrote a chapter for it herself.

Finally, to Clare who helped me with the finishing touches on the manuscript and also motivated me to go back once more.

I thank them all.

Foreword

Some years back — in 1969, if memory serves me right — I was somewhat taken aback to receive a safari inquiry from a Reverend Henry T. Folsom. A REVEREND! A PREACHER MAN! Good Heavens! On safari?

Further on in the inquiry it transpired that I had been recommended by some old friends, Justus (Butz) and Elsa Von Lengerke of Stag Lake, New Jersey. Hank Folsom's father had been a crony of Butz' father, and so Hank was considered a suitable candidate by the family.

Discreet inquiries (for one does not want this sort of thing to get about too much) among the hunting fraternity in Nairobi elicited the fact that none of my associates, except, I think, Syd Downey had ever been on safari with a man of the cloth.

So began a two-year correspondence, and in 1971 at Embakasi Airport (the old one, before Jomo Kenyatta Airport) in Nairobi I met Hank and his two sons, Henry and Randy.

Having been to a school in England that was in the shadow of Canterbury Cathedral, I was naturally rather in awe of people who wore their collars backwards. I treated them with the sort of suspicion reserved nowadays by the youth for the police.

I need not have worried, for Hank and myself soon became firm friends. I found him to be a confirmed Anglophile; this was refreshing, as most of my American friends are pretty "anti-Brit" in their attitudes. To my delight not only was he the first and only member of the Baker Street Irregulars (Sherlock Holmes Society) I have ever known, but he liked strange foods like bitter marmalade, kippers, kidneys, marrow bones, snorkers (sausages), all dear to Colonials like myself.

Although not a "killer" (to my great joy), Hank was terribly enthusiastic, and I used to watch with amused tolerance (sometimes!) when in his enthusiasm he would crash through the undergrowth after some terrified denizen of the bush like a Rugby front-row forward (or a football linebacker).

After that first safari in Tanzania with Hank and his sons, I had the pleasure of being on safari, in Kenya this time, when Hank brought his wife, Phyllis, along. Then they were on safari again in South Africa in 1983, in Botswana in 1987 and Zambia in 1990. On his Zambian safari Hank and Phyllis had their grandson, Charles, along so I had the satisfaction, once again, of hunting with three generations of one family. In 1993 I did my last safari with Hank. This time we spent three weeks in Tanzania's South Masailand looking for a decent buffalo and a hairy lion. Since this 1993 safari Hank has made a second trip to South Africa and is planning yet a third in 1999.

Hank was greatly inspired by his father's diary of a safari he had undertaken as quite a young man in Kenya in 1913 — a small book filled with the most tiny writing. Although Hank has covered a tremendous amount of ground in Africa after seven safaris — from the Tana River in Kenya down through Tanzania, the Luangwa Valley and Lake Bangweulu in Zambia to the Chobe and Savuti in Botswana and on to South Africa — he will never have the experiences that his father did in those six months with George Outram on an ox wagon safari in Kenya. Africa has changed so much, even in the 27 years since Hank's first safari, and just as Hank will never have the experiences his father did, so he will never again hunt the areas of his earlier safaris.

As we grow older and creakier, crankier and more deaf, I am afraid I will accompany Hank no more on safari when we can sit around the campfire (Hank always said that was *the* best time of the day) and listen to the lions roar and discuss the day's successes or failures and relive past trips. Surely the best way to travel? But Hank can go, and I wish him every success.

I feel it has been a great honor to be asked to write the foreword for *Rendezvous In the Bush*, and I pen these words with great respect and pleasure for my friend.

I could go on and describe the various trips we did together, but that's not my job — so over to Hank.

David Ommanney
Old Fort, North Carolina
August, 1998

Introduction

In recent years the general reader has been able to recover much of the history of African hunting during the 19th and 20th centuries, as well as many of the incredible adventures involved in the exploration and settlement of East Africa where it all began. Quite a few of the books about and by the early pioneers have been republished, and some of the more recently retired professional hunters have been writing autobiographical accounts of taking their clients into the bush. Anyone who has ever tasted the actual experience of such a Safari — or even dreamed about it — has to be deeply grateful that these records of African settlement and of the glory days of its hunting are now safe for future generations to enjoy and to relive vicariously.

I hope the reader of this modest work by a rank literary amateur will understand that my African knowledge and experience is very limited and that what follows cannot be compared with those classics either in style or content; it is simply an attempt to keep alive one client's happy memories of some adventures over 26 years and which can never be repeated.

It started in August, 1971 when I took my two sons on safari in Tanzania. Shortly after our return I wrote an article, describing my greater kudu hunt: *The Gray Ghost of Africa*. However, I never tried to publish it; instead I simply tacked it on to my personal hunting diary.

After my next safari I wrote a piece about a buffalo hunt: *Rendezvous In the Bush*; this too was added to the hunting diary. However, after three more trips and reading so many of the current books of the recollections of both professional hunters and their clients, I thought I would try my own hand at it.

So I used my two unpublished pieces as a nucleus for a short book on my philosophy of hunting, a few of my own reminiscences, and some of my fears and hopes for the future of Africa's incomparable fauna.

I thought this *magnum opus* was finished after the 1990 trip. However, three years later I took still another safari — a largely sentimental one in Tanzania with my old professional and friend, David Ommanney. This time I purposely did a minimum of shooting, but it still meant that my supposedly completed literary effort would need some editing and a few more pages. So, *The Year of the Buffalo,* and for good measure, a chapter on African bird shooting were added. But then, as the reader will see, there was still more: a paradoxical safari to South Africa with my new wife, Clare, in 1997. Now it looks as though there is going to be still one more African hunt, but I cannot postpone the final writing of these reminiscences any longer. *Tempus fugit!*

Henry T. Folsom
Randolph, New Hampshire, 1998

Chapter 1

Apologia

AFRICA: What does this word mean? For some it is a place of origin, a land from which a culture was wrenched over a period of 300-400 years when thousands of black tribesmen were sold by their own people to slavers. These slavers in turn herded the men in great caravans of misery to the east coast, and subsequently into the Arab lands of the Middle East. Sometimes they were taken by force from West Africa, chained together, and then transported under unspeakable conditions to labor as slaves on the sugar plantations of Cuba and the Caribbean, planting and cultivating cotton or tobacco in our antebellum South. If they were more fortunate, they served at tables in the great mansions of that era. For their descendants the Africa of today is becoming a place from which a culture is gradually being recovered through the mists of time and history.

AFRICA: Does it bring back visions of great explorers who braved hunger, fever, hostile natives, the "great thirst" in the heat of the desert in southern Africa, or the drenching and rotting rain forests of the Congo in the west? There was David Livingstone, who discovered Victoria Falls and Sir Henry M. Stanley who first traveled the length of the Congo River to Lake Albert and ultimately confirmed John Speke's discovery of the Victoria *Nyanza* as the true source of the White Nile. Perhaps, above all others, it is this search for the origin of the world's longest river that captures our imagination and is most remembered in African exploration.

AFRICA: Does the word bring to mind a desert, the great Sahara with its own subculture — the Arab world of Islam? We may envision isolated outposts of the French Foreign Legion, or the inexorable southern advance of Kitchener's Victorian regiments, driving the Mahdist followers of the Khalifa Abdullah toward their final destruction at Omdurman. From more recent times the term evokes memories of great tank battles, raging across the sands and around the arid hills of the north: Tobruk, El Àlamein, the Kasserine Pass, Hill 609.

AFRICA: Perhaps it is the south where three great cultures met head-on in deadly collision: The Victorian imperialists, personified by Cecil Rhodes; the Dutch-descended Boers, led by Oom Paul Kruger; and the Bantu tribesmen under Shaka Zulu, who created the greatest aboriginal empire in African history. It was Cetshwayo, a later Zulu king, forced into a war he did not want, whose *impis* virtually wiped out a British force of over 950 well equipped and supposedly well-led troops along with an equal number of Natal *Kaffirs* at Isandhlwana in 1879. Of course, the British exacted the final and inevitable price at Ulundi six months later when the old Zulu order disappeared amid the ashes of the king's *kraal*. This great cultural conflict is even now approaching its violent denouement in South Africa's tribal strife and the struggle within majority rule.

AFRICA: Does the word remind us of the frightening ecological threat of a population growing at a rate of four percent a year while at the same time the uninhabitable Sahara is ever creeping southward; of a land where even now there is not enough food and where there will soon be still less? Does it connote newborn nations, struggling to survive within the international community against incredible internal handicaps that are largely engendered by a lack of arable land, a propensity for corruption inherited from generations past, and the inherent tribalism that is still such a part of black Africa?

AFRICA: Do we think of the misnamed "Dark Continent," the land of tooth and claw, as the greatest assemblage of wild animals on earth, which is now making its last and probably hopeless stand against advancing "civilization" with its unquenchable thirst for *Lebensraum*? This is the land of the lion, the leopard, the African elephant, the Cape buffalo, the elusive bongo, the greater kudu, and the pathetic remnants of the once numerous rhino that have been harried and hurried toward extinction by man's greed. This is the Africa of the hunter. It is really the only Africa I have ever known, and it is the Africa with which I have a love affair that will not die. What follows is about that Africa —

the Africa of the safari — specifically the classic big game hunting safari.

Since before the dawn of history Africa has been a hunter's paradise. It is not coincidental that human life seems first to have evolved around Lake Rudolph in Kenya and a bit later at Olduvai Gorge in Tanzania. Game was in such abundance that primitive hunters, even with the crude weapons then available, were able to secure meat. Protein-starved people today still hunt antelope, zebra, and even elephant to meet this need. Unfortunately, however, too many also hunt the elephant for its "white gold," ivory, which is sold throughout the world's black market; and the rhino for its horn, used in Yemeni dagger hilts or as an alleged aphrodisiac in the Orient. We can only hope that the latter's recent addition to the endangered species list and a ban on the sale of ivory may help. But it may be too little and too late.

The first people to pursue the game other than for food were those intrepid Europeans of the 19th century who hunted anything that roamed with that day's most unreliable muzzle-loading rifles of immense size. Sir William Cornwallis Harris led the way into the bush country of southern Africa early in the 19th century. He was followed by men like R. Gordon Cumming, William Charles Baldwin and William Cotton Oswell. Somewhat later perhaps the greatest hunter of all — Frederick Courteney Selous, whose books are still classics in many of the world's hunting libraries — forged his way northward into what is now Zimbabwe, Botswana and Zambia.

Then late in the last century and early into our own — while the country still teemed with game — a new figure appeared on the African scene: The commercial ivory hunter. Some of these men made fortunes — and generally lost them — in the ivory trade, in some cases taking thousands of tusks to market throughout their careers. Their names are legendary: William Finaughty, Arthur H. Neumann, "Mickey" Norton, Bill Buckley and Quentin Grogan, among others. Perhaps the greatest of all the ivory hunters was Walter D. M. *"Karamoja"* Bell, who continued hunting well into the 20th century. His uncanny knowledge of the whereabouts of an elephant's brain enabled him to kill far in excess of 1,000 animals, usually using such unlikely calibers as the light .275 and the even lighter .256. However, he emerged unscathed and eventually retired to a comfortable and well-heeled old age in Scotland. He not only knew where to find the elephant's brain but he knew when to quit.

About the time profitable ivory hunting began giving out just prior to World War I, there was a rebirth of sport hunting. However, instead of English gentlemen such as Harris, Baldwin, or Selous setting up their own safaris, an industry began to emerge. Out of this a remarkable group of people appeared — the professional hunters. These men did not hunt for themselves. They were hired by wealthy clients from Europe and America for a most extraordinary experience — the classic hunting safari. There are too many names for any comprehensive list here, but some should be mentioned. First, very early in the 20th century was R. J. Cunninghame. He was followed by such unforgettable characters as Bill Judd, who hunted with Theodore Roosevelt in 1909; Philip Percival later of Ernest Hemingway fame; George Outram, who took my father out in 1913; Syd Downey and Donald Ker, Denys Finch-Hatton and Bror von Blixen-Finecke, Charles Cottar and J. A. Hunter. In more recent years there have been Tony Dyer, Harry Selby, Brian Herne, Dave Lunan, Tony Archer, David Ommanney, Jackie Blacklaws, Glenn Cottar, Reggie Destro, Tony Henley, and many others; so the list goes on. In 1934, The East African Professional Hunters Association was formally created by those who earned their living by taking clients into the bush. This was during the dying days of the British Empire just prior to World War II. In its 44 years of existence this association had a tremendous influence on the intelligent hunting and management of wildlife. When it was disbanded in 1978 the game in East Africa came in for very hard times.

After the hiatus caused by the Depression and World War II the Golden Age of modern hunting safaris in East Africa dawned. It only lasted for about 30 years — but what a 30 years! — and it virtually ended with the closure of hunting in Kenya in 1977. There is still some going on in Tanzania, and for a while longer there will be hunting — even good hunting — in some other parts of the continent, but the day of the classic safari is gone with the wind. I count myself fortunate to have experienced it in Tanzania in 1971 and in Kenya in 1975 as the last flicker of twilight of that old Africa was vanishing. Since then I have hunted in Zululand and the Transvaal, Botswana, Zambia, and Tanzania again, but these latter hunts have made me realize only too painfully that the glory days are gone forever.

How sad it is that in a few short years we may no longer hear the maniacal cry of the hyena, no longer be able to watch elephants washing and spraying in the Tana or Chobe Rivers, no longer marvel at vast herds of wildebeest and zebra working north out of the Serengeti into the Masai Mara. Perhaps the greatest loss will be when we are unable to sit around a campfire under the Southern Cross and hear the lion's roar, the most unforgettable sound of the African night. As the human population continues to grow and as inoculation against the tsetse fly, and even its eradication, enables people to take their cattle into the "fly area," which is at present the game's last natural refuge, there just will not be any room left. Of course, people must come first; they have to live, but one would like to think that a few corners of the vast continent of Africa might remain where the game could live free.

At least those of us who were there will always have our memories: Memories of a long stalk under the African sun for some elusive antelope; memories of moving oh-so-carefully with a pounding heart into the brush after a wounded lion or buffalo; memories of finally dropping the greater kudu, the Gray Ghost of Africa, at the last moment of daylight on the last day of safari.

However, the actual hunting is only part of it — perhaps even a small part of it. It is the intoxication of drinking deeply from the waters of Africa, the cheerful *"hodi"* at the tent door very early in the morning, and a hot cup of tea before reluctantly emerging from the warmth of a comfortable bed. It is the cough of the engine in the bone-chilling cold of the African predawn, followed by a gradual and welcome warming as the sun comes over the horizon and then moves higher into the sky. It is the relaxation of the hot shower after a long day's hunt; it is the cold drink around the campfire under Africa's night sky with the stars so bright it seems you can almost reach out and touch them. This and so much more is the stuff of the classic hunting safari, which is now gone, but which, once having been experienced, can never be forgotten.

Why the *hunting* safari? Why must blood be shed? When I talk about my trips to Africa, I hear this question more than any other, and there is probably no answer which will satisfy those who are strongly opposed to all hunting. I can respect their feelings; I hope they will respect mine. Unfortunately there is a deepening gulf, not so much between hunters and non-hunters as between hunters and *antihunting groups*. Because of the growing political clout of the latter and ever-increasing pressure for gun-control laws (which, let us admit it, are in *some* cases probably warranted) hunting will become more difficult. Being a bit cynical about the motivation behind some of these attempts at gun-control, I would observe that while the increasing restrictions on ownership and use of firearms does not appear to be reducing crime, it will probably prove a most effective means of eliminating hunting. So gradually the antihunting groups seem to be winning out; it is just a matter of time.

If really pressed, a few of these people will sometimes grudgingly admit that perhaps controlled hunting may benefit the *species* by preventing over taxation of the environment's capacity for food production. However, they cannot — rather they *will not* — understand why such control cannot be left to game wardens and government employees; let *them* cull the herds down to manageable size. In other words why should the ordinary citizen *want* to hunt and kill animals that have done him no harm and that he does not really need for food? After all, he could keep himself (or herself) in a liberal supply of prime beef for many, many years on what a 30-day safari in Africa costs.

Many people assume that hunters are heartless people who take pleasure in killing and even in the sadistic inflicting of pain on defenseless creatures — "butchers," they are sometimes called. I am sorry to say that this is true in some cases. There are game hogs who simply want to shoot and kill as much and as often as possible. These "sportsmen" are an abomination, and they cross all socioeconomic lines. There is the "redneck bubba" who goes into the woods with a gang of companions for a weekend of beer drinking and "huntin'." They organize a drive that leaves a deer little chance. After executing an unfortunate buck that tried to run the gauntlet, our great hunter then carries it around on his pickup truck — sometimes for days —

with his trusty rifle prominently displayed for all to see on the gun rack behind him. In effect this "slob hunter" is saying, "Look what a macho guy I am!"

There is also the multimillionaire "sportsman" whose life revolves around the next trip and all the shooting and killing it will bring. He may even hold an Alaskan or African guide on retainer to phone or fax when some especially good trophy is spotted — often denying the client of the moment the opportunity of hunting it. Within 24 hours our wealthy Nimrod has flown away in his Lear Jet to wherever that trophy is. He pots it, perhaps even "tally ho-ing" it — chasing it down and shooting it from a safari car window — then returns to his business the following day to await the next blowing of the horn of the hunter. Granted, both these examples may seem a bit extreme, but the first is common, and the second not unknown. Neither is a real sportsman, and if all hunters were like this, I for one would be in the vanguard to abolish the sport entirely.

Yes, we must concede much abuse, and not just in recent times. Africa's game has been ruthlessly hounded, trapped, poached, and slaughtered over the last 100 years and, if anything is going to be left, all sportsmen have an obligation to work toward the stopping of this *wanton* killing of so much of her irreplaceable wildlife. Rigid anti-poaching laws must be enacted and *enforced*; penalties must make it simply too costly for people to poach — especially for financial gain. Careful game management must be employed to insure that even in the case of legitimate and licensed hunting no species is overshot.

Whatever criticism may be aimed at the recent socioeconomic policies of South Africa, it has to be admitted that they have been handling their game very well. After virtually wiping it out in the last century, they suddenly awoke to the fact that they were destroying a valuable financial asset. Game ranching, the raising and harvesting of wild animals as a crop, has become very profitable on ranches in Zululand, the Transvaal, and the Great Karroo in Cape Province. Today the survival of South African game is assured, at least and until some future government adopts a different policy.

In most of Africa — especially in East Africa — wild game is regarded by the native population as a liability. The little farmers, those

The author with a Masai bushbuck taken near Narok (Kenya) in 1975.

After some bad shooting earlier in the 1971 safari, this one-shot kill topi restored the author's confidence.

Typical trophies from the Great Karoo and South Africa (1983): Gemsbok (above) and Bontebok (below). With good game ranching, these trophies will now survive in the wild.

scratching out a living on their *shambas*, see kudu, buffalo, and other plant-eating animals as a threat, as competition with their herds of cattle over what natural food there is. They would be happy to see *all* the game disappear. It would be wonderful if only they, too, might be convinced that properly controlled wildlife can be an asset, a source of profit that would make their lives better. Then some vestige of that wildlife might survive, even as its natural habitat inevitably dwindles through the dual threats of a growing population and an increased demand for land.

Again, granting all that I have said, what legitimate pleasure can one derive from hunting and killing animals? Would it not be better simply to leave game control to the wardens and rangers? I am frequently asked how I can possibly enjoy hunting. In response, I can truthfully say that I love animals. I have always had pets (spoiled rotten), and I am a person who will stoop down to lift a bug out of a puddle in which it is struggling to survive. A Spanish philosopher on hunting once explained that one does not hunt in order to kill, but kills in order to have hunted. Why is this so? Why not simply hunt with the camera? After all, it is far more difficult taking photographs for those fantastic books on African wildlife that are so popular today than it is to go out with a high-powered rifle and telescopic sight and drop an animal 200-300 yards away. There may be no good answer to the question "Why?" Somehow I simply do not associate hunting primarily with killing. There is so much more involved: The strategy, the stalk — often under a broiling African sun or through fever-ridden swamps — sometimes the risk, often repeated failure, and then the final denouement. Of course, exactly the same can be said of photography; I cannot deny this. I enjoy photographing game immensely and as an amateur have done quite a bit of it. It is conceivable that the time may come when I will put the rifles away entirely and limit myself to photographing the wild animals, wherever that may be. As of now for me, at least, a safari entirely without the rifle would be a bit like a martini without the gin — *something would be missing!*

I admit that I cannot build a fully convincing *apologia* for trophy hunting, but I hardly feel that is necessary. Frankly, I enjoy hunting when it is done in a sporting manner and when it does not threaten the existence of some species, as it would in the case of the increasingly rare tiger in Asia. I enjoy it, and I offer no further justification. However, I ask those whose minds are not closed, but who nonetheless oppose hunting, to stop for a moment and consider the question in another light. I grant that there are some people who are ethical vegetarians, those who out of moral conviction will not eat the flesh of any animal. Personally, I think they are missing a great deal of enjoyment, but that is their decision, and I respect it. However, there are others who maintain that it is all right to eat *domestic* animals, because they are raised for that purpose and are (presumably) slaughtered in a humane manner. In one sense, at least, I believe this is even more questionable from a moral perspective, because the steer or the sheep that is led to slaughter without hope of survival has grown up trusting man. It thinks of him as its provider and friend. Then it is betrayed. This certainly is not true of the wild animal that knows only too well that man is a most efficient predator and a very real threat. Also, more often than not in a fair hunt the animal escapes. This is not true in a slaughterhouse. At the same time, as far as I can tell, the fact that the steer or sheep — or even chicken, for that matter — is a domestic animal does not make its life any less sacred or precious to it than that of a wild animal. Its death is just as final.

Trophy hunting is admittedly hunting for pleasure, and when the hunt is successful, it cannot be denied that an animal has lost its life. But to the non-vegetarian who is, nevertheless, unhappy with hunting on principle I pose one question: How does taking an animal's life for the pleasure of hunting differ *in essence* from taking an animal's life for the pleasure of eating it? Let there be no mistake; in neither case is its death necessary for the ultimate well-being of the person involved. We may, if we feel strongly about it, criticize the hunter who shoots an animal only because he takes pleasure in the sport of hunting. But if we do so, let us at least be consistent and also take issue with the gourmet diner who sits down with his friends to enjoy a juicy sirloin or a succulent lobster for precisely the same reason. These animals, too, were killed to provide pleasure *and nothing more*, because medical science has pretty well established that a balanced vegetarian diet is

11

probably healthier, or at least as healthy, as one with meat. Consequently, it follows that when we do eat meat, an animal has been killed solely to provide us with pleasure at the dinner table. *Quod erat demonstrandum.*

I have already described some of the seamy aspects of "hunting." But there is another side as well: Hunting as it should be. Whether one is setting out alone after a white-tailed deer early on a frosty New England morning, or creeping up on a lion bait at dawn, not knowing what, if anything, will be there, or hunting a Dall sheep high in the mountains of the Yukon, big game hunting can test one's patience, skill, and, in the case of dangerous game, courage. It is not so much the shooting — it really is not. Any true hunter will agree with that. Somehow, *it is being part of our natural environment, not just spectators.* This means being part of it as predators, to be sure, but predators who are there not just to kill. It is the unexpected happening at any moment; it is the anticipation of what may be found in the next clearing or over the next hill; it is the experience of fear, cold clammy fear, when going into the bush after a wounded member of Africa's "Big Five." While many sportsmen may differ with me, I believe the very epitome, the quintessence of all hunting, is — or rather, was — the classic African safari. It is this unforgettable experience that I will try to bring back in the pages that follow. For a non-hunter what I have to say will not be an explanation, much less a justification for hunting, but for those who do hunt no such explanation or justification is needed. To the latter I now say, "*Twende*" — "Let's go!"

Chapter 2

A Day In the Classic Safari

"*Hodi?*" — "May I come in?"

The quiet voice outside your tent rouses you from sleep in the very early morning. Your reply, if you can collect your wits quickly enough, is "*karibu*" — the Swahili word for "enter" or "welcome."

The tent boy then slips in with a cheerful "*Jambo, bwana, habari?*" — "Hello, sir, how are you?"

If by then you are indeed awake, your answer (no matter how hung over or awful you may feel) is "*Mzuri sana, asante*" — "Very well, thank you".

Then he replies, "*Mzuri*" — "Good" "*Chai?*" — "Tea?"

You say, "*Ndio, asante.*" — "Yes, thank you." With this morning ritual over, he leaves, and you begin to collect yourself over the hot tea he has left at your bedside. Finally, you reluctantly leave the delicious warmth of bed and hurriedly dress, wrapping up in your warmest clothes, before venturing forth to huddle and shiver by a campfire in the cold of the African predawn.

So begins a day on safari. Before long you will clamber into the hunting car with your professional hunter. The trackers are huddled in the rear, usually wrapped in blankets to keep out the biting cold. Even before leaving, you and your hunter instinctively talk in whispers, and when you do pull out, it is with that tingle of excitement and anticipation that always comes, no matter how often you have done this before.

On some days you check baits. Just before first light you creep silently into a leopard blind, peering through a peephole to see whether *chui*, the ultimate cat, is feeding on the warthog or bushbuck hanging in a tree. If nothing is there, you wait silently and motionless, never taking your eyes off it, because if the cat comes, it will come like a

13

All hunters take at least one impala. This one was hunted in 1975 in Kenya.

David Ommanney Jr. with his father's trainee, Solomon visiting with some Masai natives (Kenya, 1975).

The cleanup crew.

Taking a break in the mountains near Narok (Kenya, 1975).

ghost, and you will never hear it. Suddenly it will just be on the bait.

Perhaps even before daylight you start stalking a lion bait to see whether a big male is feeding on the stinking buffalo or wildebeest carcass hung some days before. You creep along a planned line of approach to a carefully constructed lion blind, usually guided by strips of white toilet paper previously hung on bushes to mark the way in the dark, and often on your hands and knees. Your heart pounds from a combination of physical exertion and excitement. Will *simba* and his pride be there?

On other days, bouncing over some very rough track, you notice a slight lightening in the eastern sky, and before long you can dimly see game moving in the early morning gloom — a zebra or two barking in alarm at the sight of the safari car, a herd of tommies with their tails in perpetual motion, a lone hyena, slowly moving along with a swollen stomach after a successful night's hunt, heading toward where only it knows. You may even be startled by an equally startled lion, racing across your headlights, or by an ostrich tirelessly loping along before you, always maintaining just the right speed to keep safely ahead of the car. Then as the sun gets higher and as you begin to see more clearly, you hear a sound almost as symbolic of Africa as the lion's roar — the plaintive call of the wood dove: "Coooo-cooo-coo-coo-coo-coo." Africa is stirring for the day ahead.

Within an hour the sun is warming up, and you have peeled off several layers of clothing. The trackers have emerged from under their blankets and are now standing in the rear of the safari car, watching for whatever the professional has told them you are hunting that day. Presently you may see a herd of buffalo, heading back from water, and you take off after them on foot. If you have not already shed your heavy clothing, you will soon regret it, because chasing buffalo almost always means arduous and careful stalking, involving very fast walking as you try to work around in front of the moving herd — an end run, to use a football term. Sometimes you succeed, but usually they spot you or get your wind and are off with the proverbial thunder of hooves and a cloud of dust — and what dust. Even when you are successful in heading them off, more often than not, you pass them up, because there is no trophy bull among them. If there is, you cannot get a shot,

A relaxed David Ommanney (1987).

because the big bulls always seems to feed or move in the middle of the herd, much as a trophy elephant does when it is surrounded by its *askaris*.

Usually, at this point, if you previously skipped breakfast, you are ready to return to camp and refuel on vast amounts of protein — eggs, bacon, perhaps "bangers" or "snorkers" (two wonderful British terms for sausages). Or maybe you dine on my favorite: tommy kidneys on

Burning the high grass in Zambia.

What are they talking about? It must be serious. From left: Tami Miglio, David Ommanney, John Northcote — on safari in Botswana in 1987.

Breakfast in transit on the 1971 safari.

Midday lunch (when only mad Dogs and Englishmen venture out in the noonday sun). Pictured above are my sons Henry (left) and Randy.

toast (over which I always have to fight with my professional, David Ommanney, who, despite his occasional bouts with gout, cannot resist them). Then you are ready to embark again for the day's serious hunting.

Almost anything can happen during the next few hours. If you are among the miombo trees in central or southern Tanzania, you may come upon a sable antelope, one of the kudus, or a herd of elephant. If you are hunting on the plains, there are all kinds of possibilities: Buffalo, tommy, Grant, oryx, kongoni, perhaps even a lion, stretched out in the shade of an acacia tree. You just never know, and you never tire of expecting the unexpected.

Around noon or shortly thereafter, if you are not eating lunch from the chop box somewhere out in the bush, you return to camp for a cold beer, something to eat, and a midday siesta. By now it is pretty hot. Everything is slowing down, and the camp lies simmering under the fever trees. Perhaps the tent boy is ironing the day's wash, the skinner salting hides and skulls, and almost invariably your professional is asleep in his tent. I have always been driven to distraction by what, in light of my typical American need for nonstop action, seems to be an entirely unnecessary cessation from what I came 10,000 miles to do: Hunt. The guides insist that the game is lying down, and I have to admit that every little thorn bush seems to have a tommy curled up in its small spot of shade. One exception seems to be the kudu. Your professional will sometimes deign to hunt it in the early afternoon, but that, or an invasion of safari ants into camp, is about all that will drag him out right after lunch.

I have never been able to ascertain whether or not it is indeed useless to go in search of other game at that time of day. But of one thing I am sure: While you *probably* will not see very much on the plains or even in the savannas when the sun is high, nonetheless, it is absolutely *certain* that you will not find anything while sitting around camp or napping in your tent. Parenthetically, I remember the time when my wife and I were in the Masai Mara to watch the wildebeest migration before starting out on a hunting safari. It just happened that in the space of 15 minutes we saw two rhino, a cheetah, and a lion on the prowl — all at midday. So much for the alleged animal inactivity

When natives look for a bit of honey, the prospect of stings do not matter.

around lunch and the professional's siesta time. However, in these matters it is never wise to press him; all you can do is stomp around camp, looking worried, while he slumbers peacefully — or you can be sensible and take a nap yourself. Whichever you do, the result is the same: by about 4 p.m. he will be reasonably refreshed, and you will head out again to hunt until dark.

The author with his record book southern Grant's gazelle (Kenya, 1975).

If you are in the miombo, you may very well still-hunt for kudu, sitting in some abandoned native *shamba* until dusk, hoping to see the Gray Ghost slip quietly into view. Or if on the open veldt, you may cruise the plains in an effort to catch sight of a predator starting out

Almost as regular an occurrence as meals is the never-ending series of punctures. This is almost a way of life in Africa, at least it was in 1971.

on the evening hunt. You may go to investigate why the vultures are sitting on that flat-top thorn tree. Are there lions guarding a kill under it? Or you may take off on foot in pursuit of a buffalo herd.

The afternoon will pass. Perhaps you will have done some shooting, perhaps not. In either event, with the approach of darkness you begin to wend your way back to camp, tired, hot, and dusty but in a state of quiet euphoria and at peace with life.

The hunting itself may be rugged. At times it can even be dangerous. If you are out in some fly camp too far to return to your base, you may have to rough it a bit — not much, but a bit. However, never let anyone *ever* tell you that the true classic safari life at your main tented camp was anything but luxurious. We have already seen how the day started. But while you were out chasing wild beasts, camp life went on. The seven-foot bed with its soft mattress in your private tent was made up, and your dusty and sweaty clothes from the day before were washed, ironed, and placed in a neat little pile at the foot of your bed. Then when at long last you return, tired and dirty, you take a shower in a special tent out in back of your sleeping quarters with *maji moto* — hot water. This is dispensed from a five-gallon bucket, suspended from the limb of a tree, with a hose leading into the shower tent. To control the flow of water, there is a regular head on the end of the hose. However, be sparing of the water, because it is definitely not good form to run dry and have to call for a second bucket while all soaped up. After a shower you get into fresh, clean clothes and move to the newly built fire, which is already sending sparks up into the blackness of the African night. Overhead the stars are incredibly clear and bright. The Southern Cross hangs as a constant reminder that you are below the equator. Perhaps a meteor plunges down, or in more recent times a space satellite catches your eye as it moves slowly across the night sky. Iced drinks are served — whatever your poison may be — along with cashews fried in butter, buffalo marrow on crackers, or some game shish kabob that melts in your mouth.

For many people these evenings around the fire are the most memorable part of a safari. This is the time when one recounts the events of the day and hears hair-raising or sidesplitting stories from your professional's experiences with other usually nameless clients (as you trust you will be when he tells of some of *your* exploits). Sometimes you just sit quietly and listen to lions roaring over one of the baits as many as five miles away. On the old classic safari it is such moments as these that are the most unforgettable and that make the whole trip worth every dollar (many of them!) that you invested in it.

Then there is the evening meal, a gargantuan affair with a nice red or white wine, more stories, and increasing drowsiness. Afterwards it is never very long before you wander slowly, or perhaps stagger slightly, to your tent and fall into a deep and dreamless sleep — only to awaken for the whole wonderful routine again the next day.

Chapter 3

The Professional

At the heart of the Classic Safari there was, and to the degree that it still exists, there is the professional hunter. A good one can make the safari an unforgettable experience. A bad one can ruin it. I am grateful that on all my trips I have had only the former.

Hollywood has bequeathed a myth about African professionals that is almost as widely accepted as that of the U. S. Marshals of the Old West. On the silver screen the professional — until recently, "The Great White Hunter" — is always one step away from bedding down the glamorous heroine, who, incidentally, is usually in need of rescue from the omnipresent lion or leopard, pythons, crocodiles, or perhaps savage natives. Of course, our hero is always there at precisely the right moment, and it goes without saying that he never, but *never*, misses with his rifle (which, strangely enough, does not seem to have any recoil). He is also immaculately attired in proper bush clothing, complete with the traditional wide-brimmed safari hat (usually trimmed with leopard skin), gigantic Bowie knife (which, when thrown, will always stop a charging lion), and high boots.

On the other hand, the genuine article usually wears shirt, shorts, and sneakers — frequently without socks or laces. This enables him to step out of his shoes easily in order to test the temperature and freshness of buffalo, rhino or elephant dung with his bare foot. If the weather is cold, he will don a ratty old sweater. Sometimes he wears some sort of hat — not the traditional safari *chapeau*, but a fatigue cap or some floppy thing. One of my professionals affected a hat awfully close to a fedora. In short the professional hunters — the good ones — usually look most unprofessional, at least by romanticized Hollywood standards.

First of all, on a classic safari, as distinct from a weekend "quickie," the real professional must have some business sense and ability at organization because he runs a big and complex operation. It is not unusual for a client to sink between $75,000-$100,000 (or more) into a 30-day safari, and he certainly wants, and has every right to expect, that it be well organized and efficiently managed. The professional hunter (sometimes his wife, who is also apt to direct the business side of the operation) will have trained members of his crew in their duties, and that is not easy. Also, he, or again his wife, has to be a caterer who knows what to stock in food and drink in order to wine and dine the clients properly — to say nothing of feeding the crew. He must be able to organize and manage — generally through his *major domo*, the headman — a retinue of a dozen or more very specialized people. Always close to him and to his client are his highly trained trackers, who generally double as gun bearers. Along with the skinner these men are directly responsible to the professional. Someone else who reports to him is the driver of the great lorry that transports camp from one location to another. This man is usually classified as a "mechanic," but any real ability along those lines is rare indeed. More often than not out in the bush, where there are no service stations or parts departments, it is the professional who must also double as a mechanic. Then in an ascending pecking order, everyone else on the safari answers to the headman: The diggers of latrines and gatherers of fire wood; the tent boys, who are responsible for making beds and cleaning, washing, and ironing your laundry; the waiters at table, who are usually under the immediate direction of the headman, himself — replete with white jacket — and finally the cook.

So much for camp organization. Professional hunters, just because they are professionals, have all kinds of clients. There are wealthy habitues who book regularly every year. Some of these just come for the safari life, which they have grown to love. Shooting, if any, is casual, generally for camp meat. Other regulars are very serious and demanding clients who have hunted all over the world and are seeking the best trophies they can find, hoping to add even more next to their names in Rowland Ward's *Records of Big Game*, or Safari Club International's counterpart.

Others come on safari, generally with friends, simply to relax and

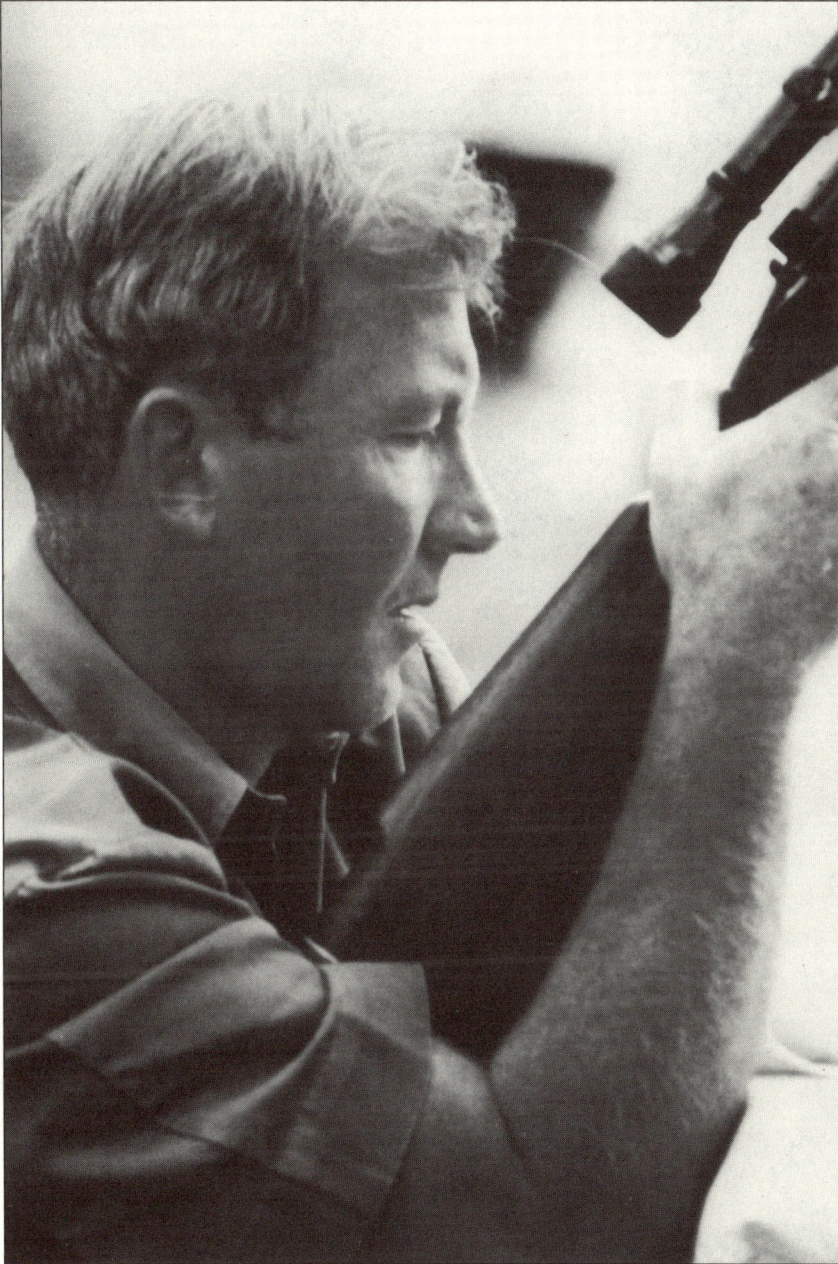

David Ommanney: My mentor and drill sergeant on numerous safaris.

drink. Their hunting is apt to be desultory, and it is not unknown for them to send out their professional to secure trophies that will eventually hang on their walls — and thereby will also hang many a wild and exciting tale.

There are no service stations in the bush. The professional hunter (Dave O.) must also be able to supervise the "native" engineers.

Dave Ommanney Jr. with his Peter's gazelle (Kenya, 1975).

Dave Sr. watches as he burns more grass in African game lands.

This is what safari life is really all about. From left: John Northcote, Tami Miglio, Dave Ommanney and Phyllis Folsom (1987 safari).

Sometimes there is the aging Nimrod, accompanied by a young beauty, who is often a newly acquired second wife, but just as frequently a "travelling companion" or office secretary, who has come along to take "dictation." Of course, our hero wants to show off his manly prowess before her with a rifle, but also in other pursuits which are best confined to the tent after dark — enough said. The professional must be able to adapt to all situations and all types of clients.

From time to time there is the newcomer, someone who has never been on an African safari and who is eager to hunt anything and everything. While he can be a trial to the hunter because of his naivete, he can also be a joy simply because of his boundless enthusiasm. The professional generally likes breaking these "first timers" into the disciplines of the safari and the hunt gradually. Incidentally, women are almost invariably easier to teach than men because they usually do what they are told without question. Whereas, because some macho male neophyte managed to bag a white-tailed deer in Maine, he is apt to think he knows it all.

The professional hunter must be a conversationalist. Most clients resent it if he keeps to himself. They expect him to sit around the campfire or mess tent, discussing anything and everything from the prospects and plans for the next day's hunt to quantum physics, politics, philosophy, or even, as in the case of my various professionals, theology! He really has to be a conversationalist, and a good one. Also, it does not hurt for him to be able to play a rubber of bridge or a game of poker. I have found that most of them abhor card games, but still they had better know how to play; they must indeed be able to adjust to all kinds of clients. For example, I used to celebrate the Holy Eucharist on Sunday mornings while on safari. David Ommanney dutifully attended, and when I asked him whether this was the first time this had happened during his career, his reply was that it was the first time in the history of the profession!

Of course, it is needless to add that the most important skill required of the hunter is an ability to guide his client to good trophies and then get him safely back to camp in one piece. This means he must be more than an adequate shot — the good ones can drive tacks at 100 yards — and he must be able to find the brain of a charging elephant from any angle. Actually, huge as it is, the bull elephant's brain presents a surprisingly small target, that is very easy to miss when several tons of pachyderm come crashing through the brush from 30 feet away.

Yes, the first requirement of a good professional has to be his shooting ability; his client's life — to say nothing of his own and the keeping of his license and reputation — depends on this. However, almost as important is his ability to locate good trophies and distinguish them from mediocre ones. Simply finding game is not enough. He must have the eye and experience to judge within a half inch or so the length of a greater kudu's horns at 200 yards in the failing light, or to within five pounds the weight of a bull elephant's tusk when it is standing in thick cover. Although he has trackers — most of whom could track a barefooted Italian across the cobblestones of St. Peter's Square on Easter morning — still he, too, must be able to decipher the signs indicated by the spoor. So he had better be a pretty good tracker in his own right.

Last, but certainly not least, the professional hunter, no matter what his age, must be physically able to keep up with his client in the bush. Usually, this is not too difficult, but once in a while some marathon runner signs on, and the professional had better be able to walk even him off his feet. He has to maintain himself in good physical condition. This is not always easy when he is also expected to keep up with his client's drinking bouts, handle tremendous meals and stay awake until the often late hours when the client may finally go to sleep. In addition he must survive the generally exhausting annual schedule that in the glory years used to keep the professional in the bush the better part of 10 months out of 12. Now that more countries are shortening their hunting seasons to nine or even six months the regimen is not quite so demanding, but it is still hard enough.

The life of the professional can be an exciting one, but also one of great tedium or even boredom. His home life is usually almost nonexistent, and it is the rare marriage that survives the years, even decades, of long and repeated absences. Strangely enough, very few professionals ever seem to have much money in their jeans. They rarely get wealthy, even though safari prices have become astronomically high. Eleven hundred dollars a day for one professional with one client in Tanzania is not unusual, and this excludes transatlantic transportation, unreal charter fees, which can run as high as $2,000 a flight, trophy fees, taxidermy and incidentals.

If you ever go on a safari — and better hurry if you are so planning — choose your professional hunter carefully. Talk to other clients who have been out with him. What kind of trophies has he brought in, and what is his crew like? Is he easy to get on with, and does he have access to good hunting blocks and concessions? If he works for a safari company, as most of them do now, check into that, too. Many a wonderful safari has been ruined by the loss or spoilage of trophies long after the client has returned home and has been waiting months for their arrival on his side of the Atlantic. I know of one instance in which an American client's trophies were misdirected by a safari company to Australia. Almost miraculously, they were traced and finally redirected properly. On one occasion I myself had a mix up on tags with someone else's beautifully mounted buffalo eventually arriving at my house. Fortunately, this error, too, was somehow corrected, and in due time I did get my own back. So check the company track record carefully; it can save you a lot of grief.

As I said before, a good professional and hunting firm can result in a wonderful and unforgettable trip. At the prices you must pay now be sure to get a really good one — he is worth it. Then, even though the so-called Golden Age is long gone, you can still enjoy the experience of a lifetime. Keep the wind in your face and good hunting.

Chapter 4

The Accoutrements

Before we get into the hunting itself, let us look at some of the equipment and accoutrements that once made up a classic safari, even though much of this is now only a fond memory. Today, safari companies generally set up permanent camps on their concessions, and you drive — or more likely fly by chartered plane — from one to another. Your professional and his trackers generally come with you, but the rest of the crew remains at its respective camp. In some of these you sleep in cabins or thatched huts rather than in the tents of the old days; you probably even have running water and flush toilets. On one trip we were in more a resort than a hunting camp — with a swimming pool no less. Times have changed, but in writing this, I am trying to recapture the memory of a Golden Age, a memory of which an occasional faint echo may still be heard in some of the more remote hunting areas in Africa.

Camp equipment consists of what can be packed on a huge lorry. This includes tents of all kinds: Tents for sleeping, a mess tent, tents for outhouses, tents for showers, tents for the crew, and even a tent to house the firearms and ammunition. There is also a gas refrigerator, a cooking stove (generally consisting of an oil drum for baking), tables, chairs, personal lockers for the client and professional, food and drink to satisfy all palates, safe drinking water that has been brought from civilization, and gasoline — petrol in Africa. Incidentally, it was the incredible rise in gasoline prices — at one point reaching $10 a gallon — that, at least in part, necessitated the switch to permanent camps. You sleep in comfortable seven-foot beds complete with sheets, pillowcases, and blankets, and you have a wash basin. In short, you are supplied with about everything imaginable to make life just as comfortable as possible after a day of hot, dusty and tiring hunting.

The cook's domain.

As mentioned earlier, for many the most enjoyable memories of safari life are early evenings spent around the campfire under the African stars. You have showered and changed into freshly laundered and ironed clothes, and now you look forward to just about any libations you want — with plenty of ice — and you can enjoy hors d'oeuvres concocted from any of many mouth-watering delicacies.

The mess tent comes with meals you might expect to find only in gourmet restaurants — at least so they seem after a long day's hunt — and it is astonishing how a good African cook can prepare food in the bush. Strangely enough, these same men often cannot perform well when introduced to a regular kitchen range back in Nairobi, Harare, or wherever your professional happens to live when he comes in from the bush. On safari nothing is left wanting — even down to a good red or white wine to go with the tilapia or Nile perch, followed by buffalo or eland steaks, chops, loin, or a good guinea-fowl curry.

Then at long last, perhaps after a cognac or two, you go to bed in an insect-proof tent. You are lulled to sleep by the sounds of the African night. These are sounds you will remember the rest of your life: The "woof" of the hyena, the cry of the bush baby, the indescribable grunting of the hippo, the rip saw of the leopard's call, and above all the roar of a lion somewhere out there on the dark veldt. Usually, the next sound you hear will be the "*hodi*" at your tent door, which marks the beginning of a new African day.

Your basic transportation usually consists of two vehicles (or more, when there are additional clients and professionals on the safari). First, there is the large lorry already mentioned. This carries camp equipment plus all the crew except the trackers, who ride in the back of the hunting car with the professional and his client. The latter is usually a four-wheel-drive pickup that has undergone extensive alterations for the rough travel to which it will be subjected. Heavy protective steelwork has been welded to the frame in front of the headlights and the reinforced grill for protection from the inevitable branches and thorn bushes through which the car plows while moving across country. There are gun racks behind the professional and client, and the truck bed has been altered to accommodate trackers riding immediately behind the cab. The cab is also protected by reinforced steel bars to which the trackers can cling as the vehicle lurches and careens through rough going. Behind them is the equipment needed to repair it at times of breakdown perhaps 20 or so miles out in the bush from camp. Not the least important are materials for patching tires after the inevitable punctures have rendered *hors de combat* the two spares that are always carried. Finally, there has to be room astern for bringing trophies back to camp; a quartered buffalo or eland takes up a lot of room.

Then there are the weapons of the safari. Most clients bring their

The 1975 Kenya safari yielded this waterbuck.

After years of hunting, I took this record lesser kudu on the Masai steppe country in 1993.

A comfortable tent on the Kisigo River in 1971.

The armory for the 1971 safari. From top: .22, .375 H & H Remington magnum, Model 70 .270 Winchester, and Model 70 .458 Winchester.

"Petrol in the lorry." That was in 1971 when this one vehicle carried everything needed for the entire camp.

own rifles and shotguns. I have done this twice, but customs and firearm regulations are so complex, especially in transit through Europe, that I found that hiring weapons from the professional or safari company is much simpler. Just be sure you check out the rented rifle on a target before starting to hunt.

As long as people hunt in Africa, I suppose there will be debates over the best armament. Americans generally prefer bolt-action rifles, often of a smaller caliber than what Europeans favor. Professionals

The Classic Safari had some classic shower arrangements as well.

are divided between bolt-action repeaters and the traditional big doubles — "*mzinga*" (cannon), as my father used to call one he had — that so many of them have used since time immemorial. David Ommanney, now retired, but with whom I went on most of my trips, usually combined the best of both worlds. He normally carried a bolt-action rifle with the advantage of its potentially greater fire power, but in those sweaty situations when one is getting in close to dangerous game he shifted to his .470 double with its capacity for two incredibly fast shots.

Typical safari crew (1971).

The hunting car in Arusha, preparing to embark on safari (Tanzania, 1971).
My son, Henry, waits patiently in the front seat.

Again on the 1971 safari. The scene in the bush after one night in transit.

Laundry detail. This was in 1971 but in some parts of Africa it might look much the same today.

Americans and Europeans also tend to differ over their choice of calibers. The former usually aim for a vital spot, often with a surprisingly light rifle (Ernest Hemingway swore by his 30.06). On the other hand the *puka sahib* from Britain is apt to choose a heavy weapon that can break down dangerous game. After all, if you shatter a buffalo's or elephant's shoulder, it will not go far or very rapidly on three legs. Also, the danger of a charge in such cases is virtually eliminated.

Today, the usual arsenal consists of a light rifle — perhaps a .270 Winchester, 30.06, 7mm Mauser, or even the .300 magnum for antelope and other non-dangerous game. But for the dangerous ones the most popular calibers are the .458 Winchester magnum, .460 Weatherby, and the .470 Holland and Holland. If a client wants to take just one all-around weapon, he probably can do no better than the .375 magnum. This is adequate for the largest game and can even be used with solids on small antelopes; the .375 is a versatile firearm and is what I had the last time I took my own rifle. However, I must say that when faced with a charge from a buffalo, elephant, or rhino, I still would feel better with the .458 or .470. The .375 simply did not have the stopping power I wanted and I was awfully glad to have Dave backing me up with his big double, but every shooter to his own choice.

To round off the weaponry there should always be a .22 for birds and such antelope as dik-dik and small duikers. If the client wants to vary his routine and diet with some wing shooting, a 20 or 12- gauge shotgun should be included in his arsenal. This can also be used on dik-dik and even such animals as the somewhat larger Thomson's gazelle. Furthermore, when loaded with buckshot, a 12-gauge is recommended by many when faced with the unpleasant prospect of going into the bush after a wounded leopard. There probably is nothing as devastating as a load of buckshot in the face at 15 feet, but pray you never have to confirm this statement.

Chapter 5

"I Guess His Time Was Up"

In August of 1987 my wife Phyllis and I, along with our friend, Tami Miglio, went on safari in Botswana, *nee* Bechuanaland. As countries in Africa go, this former British protectorate is unusual, because it is relatively wealthy. Since the fairly recent discovery of diamonds, Botswana has changed from just another poor black nation into one that is now doing very well indeed. Along with its diamond-produced prosperity is the added advantage of a small and stable population — most unusual in Africa.

On top of this, at least until very recently, it was a hunter's paradise. Sadly, there was a time when desert game and black-maned lions abounded in the Kalahari, but now that part of Botswana has had to be closed — hopefully only temporarily — because of over-hunting. However, an area north, the great Okavango Swamp, is still known for its multitudes of buffalo, sable, kudu, lechwe, lion, leopard, and a lot more. Still further north is the Chobe River that shares many of the same species with the Okavango as well as sitatunga. Until most recently the swamp and river areas also teemed with tsetse fly, the best friend African game has. Unfortunately for the wild animals, war has been declared on the fly, and perhaps for the first time in African history there is some promise of success. In the month we spent on the Chobe I was bitten only once, whereas in former years the daylight hours in fly country were spent in constant and largely futile slapping at those wicked dive-bombers. It was in Botswana some years back that the well-known professional, Jackie Blacklaws, died from sleeping sickness, which can be transmitted by tsetse. However, that is most uncommon. Virtually all tsetse bites, maddening as they are, are harmless to human beings and wild life, but the fly is absolutely deadly to domestic animals unless they are inoculated. The result has been

1983, South Africa. The author with a bush pig.

Kenya has a good population of fringe-eared oryx. This one was taken in 1975.

that until most recently in those parts of Africa where tsetse abounded, the local citizenry stayed out, because they could not bring their cattle in. When there are neither resident people nor cattle around, the game does well. However, with living and grazing space giving out, the Botswana government is seriously trying to eradicate this friend of the wild animals through aerial spraying, and cattle inoculation is also becoming more common. All this is bad news for game.

In addition, the game has been hammered hard by hunters, mostly the homegrown variety, who are taking a terrible toll on it. But it must be admitted that sports hunters have also caused a noticeable depletion in good trophy heads. It is getting much harder to find the beautiful black maned lions of the past. One reason for this is that "tally-hoing" has become common in Botswana, especially in the Kalahari, where the ground is open and flat. This is one reason hunting was closed there. Unscrupulous professionals whose clients do not care how they do their shooting (it takes two to tango) literally run the animals down in hunting cars by chasing them to the point of exhaustion. They are thus brought to bay and often as not shot from the safety of a car window — great sport. Incidentally, this abominable practice is also still common in the Sahara, where the usual prey is the addax now that the scimitar oryx has been driven almost to extinction. In a way it is even worse there, because those animals generally travel in groups, so whole herds are chased, and those which escape the "hunter's" bullet will often die from the dehydration, resulting from their desperate running in the desert sun. This type of "hunting" is so despicable that even before it was closed in the Kalahari, a number of decent professionals were reluctant to take clients out there. More power to them.

However, where we were hunting on the Chobe, the game was still in pretty good shape. I had engaged John Northcote, a veteran from East Africa who had spent his golden years there, first as a professional and then as a control hunter employed by the Game Department for game cropping. He now lives in Zimbabwe and until his recent retirement hunted both there and in Botswana. While Phyllis and Tami were not hunting, they did need a safari car for photography and game watching, so we also had Dave Ommanney as a second

John Northcote with the author's record sable (1987).

professional. While in business for himself, Dave had previously taken me out twice in East Africa on an old-fashioned safari — to Tanzania with my two sons in 1971 and then to Kenya in 1975 with Phyllis and two friends of ours from Connecticut. He probably knows Tanzania better than any modern professional. In his book *Tanzania Safaris,* Brian Herne, one of Dave's colleagues, speaks of him as being the most knowledgeable professional on Tanzanian hunting areas. However, the future of hunting in East Africa was becoming more and more dubious. So some years after my first two safaris and after the closing of hunting in Kenya, he shifted his operations first to the Sudan and then further south into Zambia, where he again established his reputation as one of the very best. As a result Dave was still hunting there, but because of very short notice had been unable to get the necessary professional's license to allow him to hunt in Botswana. Consequently, he had to limit himself pretty much to driving the girls around for photography and game watching, although he did manage to accompany John and

Like father, like son. My son, Randy, with his sable in 1971 (Tanzania).

me on a few of my hunts as well. Incidentally, in 1993 Dave decided to return to his old stamping grounds in Tanzania, where he was again licensed as a professional hunter until his retirement in 1996.

A little over halfway through our Botswana safari we were camped at Motsaudi on the edge of the great plains a few miles south of the

Chobe River. During the rainy season these plains are under water, but when we were there, in the midst of a terrible drought, they were high and dry. However, there were also little "islands" with growths of trees, dotting the hard plain and which during the rainy season were true islands.

One afternoon John and I were driving slowly over the plains, looking for whatever we might find. We had seen some zebra, but little else. Then as the sun was getting lower, he spotted something moving a mile or so away. Stopping the truck and putting his glasses on it, he simply said, "Sable."

Many people argue that the sable is the most beautiful of all African antelope, its only possible rival being the greater kudu, the Gray Ghost of Africa. There are three subspecies of sable. In the Shimba Hills at the extreme southeastern corner of Kenya there are a few survivors of the somewhat smaller East African subspecies. The larger typical race, however, is found throughout central Tanzania and south and west into Malawi, Zambia, Zimbabwe, Botswana, South Africa, and Angola. In Angola there is also — or at least there was before the civil war, which is still going on sporadically — the royal, or giant sable, which is now probably extinct. This animal was extraordinary. The largest East African specimen on record has horns 40 inches long. The number one typical sable in Rowland Ward's *Records of Big Game* is 60¾ inches (number two drops down to 55⅜ inches — not bad, however). But the number one royal sable is 64⅞ inches with *the next 24 over 60 inches*. Whether any of these glorious animals have survived is very doubtful, but we can always hope.

All the subspecies share the beauty of Africa's finest. They are among the larger antelopes in body, and the bulls are jet black with some white in their facial markings and on the underbelly. But it is the sight of their great horns, sweeping back over their topside and rump that can never be forgotten. In addition to its beauty it shares another characteristic with its cousin, the roan (larger in body, but with much shorter horns), and its more distant relatives in the oryx family. When wounded it can be extremely aggressive and has been known to charge hunters if pressed too closely. None of these animals has much to fear from predators; too many lions have found themselves skewered on the horns of sable or oryx.

John had spotted this sable bull while he was still a long way off, but we had a dilemma. In the first place he really should not have been there at all; in the south the sable is most often found in the mopanes. But there it was, way out on the open plains. Yet without driving, which we would not do, it seemed to be virtually impossible to get near enough for a reasonable shot. There was no cover behind which to stalk, so it would certainly see us before we got to within 600 yards. But then as we watched from the shelter of one of the "islands," we could see that he was ambling along very slowly, apparently with no particular purpose in mind and at an angle which might bring it past us. But the bull would still be too far away for a safe shot with the four-power scope I was using. At least he was moving in a pretty straight line, and we could tell that he would probably go by us 500-600 yards away on the far side of another "island." How could we possibly get into position and close enough for a shot? I suggested that if we waited until he passed behind the "island," we might be able to run to that wooded spot, getting close enough for a shot before he continued on to the plains and out of range.

At the time John was 67 years old, but he obviously has good genes. *Both* his parents were still living and in their nineties. I was 60 then, but still in pretty good shape from almost 20 years of fanatical jogging, so we gave it a try.

I was carrying the rifle while both of us ran, stooping low and trying to be as inconspicuous and quiet as possible. We half-loped and half sprinted across the several hundred yards to the "island." The sable could not see us, and we hoped he had not heard us, but we were still afraid that he might have speeded up for some reason and gotten out of range by the time we reached and then crossed the woods. Also, I was concerned that I might get so winded as to be unable to shoot accurately at what would certainly still be a fairly long shot.

When we finally got to the "island," I tried to catch my breath as we picked our way across as quietly and quickly as possible. Anyone who has done any hunting knows the thrill and anticipation that comes when you drop out of sight of a potential trophy in order to execute a stalk. Perhaps you make an end run around a herd of buffalo, creep into a lion blind on hands and knees, or as in this case simply keep a bunch of trees between us and the sable. You are never quite sure if what you are after will still be there when you finally get into shooting position. Once in 1940, while hunting with my father in Alberta, Canada, a grizzly bear apparently just vanished into thin air after we had dropped into a gully to get a bit closer. This time, however, we were pretty sure the bull would be in sight. There really was no way he could vanish on those flat plains. But he might have changed direction, or, being suspicious of something, shifted into high gear, putting too much distance between him and us. Once gone, there would be no catching up.

For once everything worked as planned, albeit barely. When we came to the far side of the woods, the bull was just passing beyond the end of the "island" and was perhaps 230-250 yards off. I did not have much time. John knew immediately that he was record class and told me to shoot. I had done some very erratic and at times poor shooting earlier in the safari, but this time I placed the bullet perfectly. The shot went through its heart, sending the animal into a very short circular run before it dropped stone dead. This is the way it should be — painless and quick.

This was a good, but not outstanding, sable, measuring 42 inches and just making the book. However, it was a four-inch improvement over the one I had shot in Tanzania in 1971, and, what is more, it had the kind of horns I especially like. Rather than describing a continuous arc above its back, these start to curve toward his stern in the usual manner, but then the last 24 inches straighten out parallel to his back. When I look at it on the wall, I cannot help but admire the beauty of this wonderful antelope, but I still ask myself what in the world it was doing out there on the plains. My old fatalistic Canadian guide might have explained it this way: "I guess his time was up."

Chapter 6

The Gray Ghost of Africa

When someone speaks of African hunting, such animals as the Big Five are what usually some to mind: Elephant, rhino, buffalo, lion, and leopard — the so-called dangerous game. Quite a bit will be said about these in later chapters, but there is another possible "grand slam," which some hunters consider at least as desirable, if not more so: The spiral horned antelope. There is some debate over just how many species there are, but all agree that there are at least six. However, most people add three more, even though these latter differ from the others in that the females grow horns. The species on which everyone agrees — even those people who contrive the scientific Latin names — start with the bushbuck with all its various subspecies. Then there is the shy and retiring nyala of Zululand and Mozambique and its distant cousin, the mountain nyala, found only in a very limited range in Ethiopia. Next there is the sitatunga, a truly aquatic mammal, with its various subspecies found in the swamps throughout much of the continent. After that comes lesser kudu, and finally its larger cousin, the greater kudu. There are the disputed three in which females have horns. First comes the bongo, which, along with the unrelated okapi, is perhaps the most elusive and hard-to-get large animal in Africa. Next is the common East African eland, with its brothers of the same species: the somewhat larger Livingstone's eland of south-central Africa and the Cape eland of the Republic of South Africa. Finally there is the giant or Lord Derby eland, of north-central and western Africa.

In various safaris I have managed to secure six of the nine: bushbuck, nyala, Livingstone's eland, sitatunga, lesser kudu, and greater kudu. This last — *tandala m'kubwa* — the Gray Ghost of Africa, is what Robert Ruark called the hunter's grail. It is the animal Ernest Hemingway hunted almost to the point of obsession. He writes of this relentless chase in *The Green Hills of Africa*, an account of the famous safari that he and his wife took in the mid-1930s.

Among all the antelope perhaps the male greater kudu alone rivals the sable in beauty and is second in size only to the various elands, weighing up to 600 pounds. He is gray in color with white stripes on his flanks. Yet with all his size and weight he can still vault a 12-foot fence from a standing start. However, it is his magnificent horns which are unrivaled by any antelope in Africa, great spiral horns reaching up through two complete curls and into a third. The largest subspecies is the southern race from which the world's record hunting trophy was *shot* — 69¼ inches. An even more extraordinary set of horns, measuring 73⅞ inches, was picked up and is now officially number one in Rowland Ward's record book. However, the East African variety does pretty well, too, — 63½ inches. Rowland Ward starts entering these at 52 inches, but anything over 49 or 50 is a very nice trophy.

Tandala is a shy and timid animal, but once the hunter has seen the glint of the setting sun reflecting off those horns, he is caught by the almost irresistible lure of this extraordinary animal. Then no effort is so demanding or exhausting to turn him back. He will be up before dawn and out until after sunset, day after day, even week after week, trying to run this phantom of the African hills to earth. He may hear a startled bark, catch a momentary glimpse of gray or the flash of sunlight on a horn, but then the gray ghost is gone. He may watch in frustrated dismay when, after hours of patient waiting or stalking, he sees a big bull lay his horns back and disappear into the bush; there is seldom a second chance that day.

It was this shadowy animal that made me work so hard on my first safari, which I took in 1971. I was accompanied by my two sons, Henry who was our photographer, and Randy, a neophyte hunter. David Ommanney was the professional. He took us into good kudu country in the scrubby forests along the Kisigo River in central Tanzania. But the safari had started slowly — well, not really *started* slowly. Both Randy and I had shot small impalas for camp meat and leopard bait, and I had gotten a pretty good sable — all on the first day. However, right after that things had petered out. A week or so later Randy and I were both still working very hard for kudu, but neither of us was having any success.

Looking for tracks. David Ommanney (1971) checks out a waterhole with his very loyal gun bearer, Salim, who once, armed only with a knife, had leaped onto a leopard that had Dave "down."

This sable antelope, taken in 1971, was the first real trophy of my African big game hunting career.

The routine was pretty well set: We would go into some native *shamba* at first light, where we usually hunted on foot for several hours, returning to camp for a midmorning breakfast. Then we would be out again — usually for other game — sometimes coming back for lunch, and sometimes eating in the bush. By late afternoon it would be back to the *shambas* for still hunting, hopefully waiting for a kudu to appear. We would sometimes see some cows and a few immature bulls, but nothing shootable. Finally, long after dark we returned disconsolately to camp. The skinner was always waiting in anticipation, but after a glance at the empty truck he would quietly turn away. None of us had much to say, and tempers sometimes flared a bit. However, our spirits invariably revived after a hot shower and sundowners around the campfire, and we would start talking over plans for the next day. Hope springs eternal.

This went on for almost two weeks. Originally, we had intended to move our camp north to Maswa, southeast of the Victoria *Nyanza* after about 10 days, but we then decided to stretch our stay on the Kisigo a bit longer. Randy's leopard permit was valid only in Dave's concession there. Also, neither of us could bear the thought of giving up on kudu. We were all discouraged, even Dave, because we had seen very little of anything in this normally excellent area. Randy lost one chance at a good bull when he had not been able to pick out quickly enough what was obvious to African eyes. Shortly after that I lost what at the time I was sure would be my only chance: While hunting with Katheka, one of Dave's trackers, I missed a bull cleanly. To be sure, it was a tough shot: The bull was facing us through some fairly thick brush from about 150 yards away. Maybe the light .270 bullet was deflected. Maybe I got buck fever; or maybe the fact that I was just coming down with what in Mexico we called the "Aztec Two Step" caused my hand to be unsteady. Whatever the reason, in a thrice he was gone, and with him my morale.

The day finally approached when we knew we would simply *have* to strike camp and move north if we were to have any time for buffalo, lion, and other plains game. There was still one day left on the Kisigo. How often that last day figures in kudu hunting. It started auspiciously enough: Shooting from a blind at dawn, Randy got his leopard, a nice

My Livingstone's eland (Botswana, 1987) had a 40 inch set of horns and ranked well into the record book.

tom. His trip was made, because he had wanted "Mr. Spots" more than any other trophy, and now he had succeeded.

That afternoon Dave and I started out for one more kudu hunt in the *shambas*. We had two gunbearers with us: Salim, Dave's tracker of long standing, who with only a knife had once leaped on a leopard that had Dave down; and Anton, a local who was working for us on the Kisigo. The latter said he knew a *shamba* where there were "always" kudu. We had nothing to lose, so we let him guide us to it.

Starting right after lunch (none of Dave's siestas this day), we really were not too hopeful, but immediately things began to look up a bit: We saw a fair eland right away. However, we passed it up without a second glance, because at that point I was not interested in eland. Little did I know how hard I would work for one 16 years later in Botswana, where I would get what would then be number eight in the Rowland Ward record book. We began climbing higher into the hills. It certainly was kudu country as described by Hemingway, but I was so discouraged at this point that I was not holding out much hope. In fact, I was really only going through the motions, while looking forward to hunting lions in the north.

We eventually reached the *shamba* Anton claimed "always" had kudu, and then walked half a mile or so to an abandoned native hut. The two gun bearers climbed up on the roof while Dave and I sat in the shade a short distance away. It was still early afternoon, and it was hot. We whiled away the hours, occasionally glassing the edge of the woods and incessantly slapping the ever-present tsetse flies, that were feasting on us royally throughout the afternoon.

Time passed very slowly; I became restless and indifferent, ruminating more about the iced martini awaiting me back at camp than about kudu. In fact, by then I had really given up, but Dave had not. As the last hour of daylight approached, he joined the others on the roof, while I stayed below and sulked. Actually, I was so sure nothing would happen that I almost hoped we would quit early and head back. I was fed up with hunting kudu that did not appear and was looking forward to the move north, where the plains game was so plentiful. Up there it would not be a matter of *whether* we would see game, but how good it would be.

Then as the sun was about to drop below the horizon, I slowly stood up to stretch my legs; we would *have* to head back to camp in a very few minutes. Suddenly, I was aware of pebbles dropping at my feet. I looked up and saw Dave frantically motioning me to come. Earlier in the safari I would have grabbed my rifle and scrambled

This zebra (1971) was the first I ever shot.

A native "shamba" near to the area where we hunted kudu (1971).

recklessly up the roof, but I had at last *begun* to learn. I quietly picked up the .270 and made my way carefully to the hut, keeping very low. When I got there, I handed the rifle up to him, and then crawled up a large limb that had been placed there in order to provide access to the roof.

When I reached them after what seemed an interminable length of time, Dave pointed into the gathering gloom. I felt a sense of panic, because I could not see what he and the others saw.

"*Where*, Dave?" I whispered quietly but helplessly. He handed me his binoculars, and then I was just able to make out some indistinct shapes far across the *shamba* at the edge of the woods. Apparently, his sharp eyes had picked up a momentary flash on the horns when the bull had raised his head in the setting sun. He said there were several cows, and that the bull was standing to the right.

"The one just to the left of the large tree?" I asked. When he nodded, I went on, somewhat dubiously, "Well, I'll give it a try, but he's a long way off, and I can hardly see him in this light." Frankly, I was not too hopeful, but I had caught a glimpse of those horns through the glasses and I simply had to try.

I settled comfortably in a prone position on the hut's roof, raised the rifle and looked very carefully through my little 2.5 power scope. The bull looked awfully small. "How far away is he?" I asked. When Dave said about 250 yards, I was incredulous. In the failing light it seemed more like 400. Fortunately, I took his word for it — after all he was the professional. My Winchester model 70 was sighted in to be right on at 200 yards, so I aimed a few inches high. At this point I could just make out its chest and neck, but not the rest of its body. This meant that for the second time I would be shooting at a bull facing me dead on (those sharp eyes had spotted us, and he was watching very closely). This would be a difficult shot at an animal that is quite slender when measured port to starboard — especially at this distance and in the failing light. Forcing myself to relax, I aimed just above the juncture of his neck and chest and then *squeezed* the trigger. The rifle cracked. For a moment the muzzle flash blinded me in the approaching darkness, and when I looked again, both the bull and the cows were gone.

As every hunter knows, some shots just *feel* right, and this had been one of them. I had aimed carefully and had not jerked the trigger or flinched. The rifle had gone off without my knowing just when it would, and that is as it should be. My one fear was that we had misjudged the range and that I had shot low. Dave thought I had missed entirely, because at the moment of my shot he had seen the bull lay his horns back and take off into the woods at full stride. Yet while I had done some very bad shooting on that safari and thus tended toward pessimism, still it had felt awfully good. I could not help but feel that maybe — just maybe — I had sneaked the bullet in.

Even though the others were obviously skeptical, we had to have a look. "Well, you may have hit him," Dave said, not very reassuringly, "but I don't think so." On that encouraging note, we set off. When we reached the spot where the kudu had been standing, it was really getting dark, but we could just make out his tracks. No blood, however. He had obviously gone off into the woods at a fast run. We followed for a few yards, and my heart began to sink; it looked more and more like another miss. Still that shot had felt right. So, following Dave, who was watching the track, I kept my eyes on the brush ahead, hoping against hope. Then there it was.

At first I thought it was only a large twisted branch that had fallen to the ground. But when I took that quick second look that hunters so often do in a momentary and passing surge of hope, fully expecting that I would then see that it was indeed a branch fallen to the ground, I could tell that it was *tandala m'kubwa*, the Gray Ghost. I touched Dave's arm and pointed silently. When he raised his eyes and saw the kudu, we were not absolutely certain it was dead; perhaps it was only down. Very carefully, we worked our way around a bush for a better look, but then there was no doubt.

I had never been close to a kudu before; I simply could not believe the magnificence of those horns, and my emotional reaction was something I find difficult, if not impossible, to describe to anyone who has never hunted. After so many disappointments and so much doubt, the realization that I had finally succeeded brought a flood of emotions: Immense relief, awe in the presence of such a wonderful animal, gratitude and upon reflection, as always, a bit of sadness. But even this last was mingled with great exultation.

The long kudu hunt was finished, and a sense of peaceful euphoria settled over me. For the first time this elusive phantom of the African hills had become reality for me; it was no longer simply a momentary glimpse of gray or a startled bark on the edge of a *shamba*. It was no longer a maddening source of frustration and anguished thoughts of what might have been. Now it was lying there quietly and in great dignity, shot cleanly through the heart with only the slightest drop of blood on its chest to show where the bullet had struck.

Despite my *apologia* at the beginning of this work, if the reader has managed to read this far, I am sure that there are still some who think it inhuman if not bestial to slay such an animal. Why not simply photograph it? As stated earlier, I cannot and will not try to convince them otherwise. I will only say that it did not seem then or now in the least inhuman, much less bestial. In one sense this animal has been immortalized. I do not say this simply because it would eventually be mounted and hang on my wall. No, this beautiful creature, whose normal course would have been to live a few more years and then to be pulled down by wild dogs or hyenas when too weak to flee any longer — to be disemboweled and eaten while still alive — now lives forever, indelibly planted in my memory.

Had I not been there, he would have passed on to another hill and then to another, until eventually and inevitably he would have fallen in the ruthless and unforgiving struggle between predator and prey. Then the rains would have come and washed away his tracks without a trace — for Africa leaves no traces. He would have been gone forever. In a way that I cannot explain rationally, I believe he has been spared such a fate and granted something better.

So I was able to gaze on this fallen monarch with respect and satisfaction. The Gray Ghost was dead, and somehow I felt that this was as it was meant to be.

Chapter 7

"You Shot Too High"

With the exception of Ernest Hemingway's classic *Green Hills of Africa* in which he recounts several failures, especially with greater kudu, it is rare indeed to find anything but success stories in the plethora of hunting reminiscences that are flooding the literary sports market today. Of course, one likes to remember the successes, but they are only part of the story. If the hunt were always successful, there would be very little excitement in it, and very little to write about. However, this is not the case. Even in this day of high-powered rifles and variable telescopic sights, the hunter still fails almost as often as not. Either the animal gets away without a shot being fired, or it is missed. Unfortunately, there are also instances of wounded game escaping, but in Africa, at least, this is not very common, because the code rightly insists that no wounded animal may be abandoned until every effort has been made to track it down and finish the job. Only when all hope has been lost, or when it has become apparent that the animal will recover because the wound is not fatal, can the chase be broken off ethically.

Even though one is disappointed at losing a possible trophy, such occasions are not always failures in every sense of the word. Some of the most exciting sporting experiences I have had resulted in the loss of what I was after. I will never forget the day in Casco Bay, Maine, when I fought a seven-foot blue-fin tuna that must have run over 700 pounds for two and a half hours under a hot August sun, only to have it finally get under the keel and part the line. I was terribly disappointed, but it was a fair fight, and the fish won. Today I can look back on that afternoon with great pleasure, even though I would still like to have "boated" it. Since the day in 1937 when I successfully shot my first white-tailed spiked horn in Nova Scotia with my father, I have had a number of failures in the hunt, most of them in Africa. So, with regrets over what might have been, I will relate my tale of woe about "the big one that got away" — the day the elephant won.

About the third or fourth day into my 1971 safari, I had an experience for which I really was not ready or prepared at the time. My two sons and I were with Dave Ommanney near the Kisigo River in Tanzania. One morning shortly after that auspicious first day, which had made me think African hunting must be awfully easy, Dave was casually investigating some pretty devastated trees — more out of curiosity than anything else — when he heard the sharp crack of one going down. It sounded almost like a rifle shot, and this could only mean one thing: Elephants were still around and were at work.

When a professional takes on a client as green as I was, he wisely tries to steer him clear of dangerous game until he has sized him up and the neophyte has gotten over his case of nerves and a bit used to shooting in the African bush. However, on this particular day we had practically stumbled on a herd of elephants. Dave soon caught sight of them, as did I, but apparently they had gotten a whiff of us and were already running. This was the first time I had seen elephants outside a zoo or circus, and even now I can remember how this particular herd reminded me of a freight train as it hurried past us in single file through the miombo trees. We were within a 100 yards of them, but Dave simply said, "Don't shoot," so I did not, but in my inexperience I might otherwise have been tempted.

Apparently, they were not too alarmed, because after a trumpet or two they seemed to quiet down. Dave had seen the track of a big bull. I am not absolutely certain this fellow had actually been with the herd, although it certainly seemed to have been. However, bulls do not usually mix with the cows, except when mating. Whatever the case, there was obviously a big one in the immediate area, so Dave decided to risk a hunt, even with such a tyro as myself, and the stalk began. I do not recall seeing the herd again, but he knew it was not far away, because before long we could hear the low rumbles that always signify close proximity to elephants. Until quite recently professional hunters and scientists alike believed that these were caused by sounds issuing from the stomachs of contented elephants; the rumbles always stop

David Ommanney with his own sable also taken during 1971.

the moment the herd is alerted to danger. Recent studies have shown that they actually originate in the vocal chords and are a means of communication between elephants. In fact, experimenting with tame ones, recording these sounds with special equipment has made it pretty clear that they "speak" in a range of sounds, most of which are pitched too low for the human ear to hear. It is speculated that this is the way a whole herd, when alarmed, will suddenly move at the same instant and in the same direction without any apparent signal being passed between them.

At this point we began to crawl — Dave, my two sons, the trackers, and myself; it was hard going through very thick brush. I was too new, or too stupid, to be nervous, but I certainly was getting tired, inching along, trying my best to keep quiet, and at the same time making sure that no dirt got into the muzzle of the .458 I was lugging. Green as I was, right from the start I should have known that something was imminent when the gun bearer handed the rifle to me.

63

Then Dave stopped and pointed directly ahead. Right there, not more than 20 yards away, a large bull was towering over us. I still was not frightened, and I did not act impulsively. I raised my rifle slowly and aimed very deliberately directly between his eyes for a brain shot. He had not seen us — an elephant's eyesight is not good — and the wind was right, so the bull had not smelled us either. However, he must have heard something, because he was obviously suspicious and was stretching his trunk toward us, trying to catch our scent. Then I fired.

I may have been inexperienced at that point, *but at 20 yards I do not miss what I am aiming at.* So the instant I pulled the trigger, I relaxed and waited for him to collapse. Instead, he only slumped, then whirled and started to run. Dave and I were both so astonished that it took a second or two to react. I did finally pump a second cartridge into the chamber, and we both fired at about the same time, but it was too late. The bull had gotten into the brush and was gone.

We knew the bull had been hit, so of course we started off on his track. Dave could not understand how I had missed at that range, so he asked just where I had aimed. I told him on a line between the elephant's eyes. He groaned and simply said, "You shot too high." The bullet had gone above the brain and through a great honeycomb of bone. Apparently, at the moment I fired the elephant was tilting his head back and reaching out with his trunk. Because of this, I should have aimed about six inches *below* the eye in order to hit the brain. Had I done this, the boys would have had several hours' hard work, cutting out what Dave estimated to be about 80 pounds of ivory in each tusk. As it was, he was not at all confident that I would get a second chance with this bull.

We followed the tracks under a very hot sun for about three hours. At first there was a fair amount of blood that had brushed off on the leaves and branches as the bull plowed through them; so tracking was fairly easy. Also, he had quickly developed diarrhea — the result of shock and nerves — but this did not last long. Very soon the dung was normal, and the bleeding from his forehead had stopped. However, he had not calmed down sufficiently to slow up, and continued to move at a pace just about twice what we could maintain. Finally, after

Bwana Mzee: Everyone lets his beard grow — at least once. I quickly shaved it off after learning that *Bwana Mzee* meant "Old Man!"

about three hours when Dave saw that it was hopeless, we broke off pursuit.

Of course, I was disappointed, and still am, but in retrospect I realize now that the bull, instead of turning and fleeing, could just as easily have come for us from 20 yards. What would have happened then I cannot say, so perhaps it is just as well things turned out as they did. Dave assured me that after suffering from a pretty bad headache for a few days, the elephant would recover completely; in any case he certainly made good its escape.

Later in the safari I had one more chance; we were again close to elephants — so close that we stood motionless next to a sleeping herd for an hour or so. We were in thick woods and not more than 20 or 30 yards from them. One bull, standing broadside at that, had a very nice tusk visible to us, but Dave simply could not see the other and did not want me to shoot for fear that he might be a mono-tusker. Consequently, we waited without moving until they awoke and began to stir. Then when the big fellow turned, we could see that he did indeed have two good tusks. But at that very moment, as so often happens, a treacherous breeze puffed up; they caught our scent and fled in a blind panic, screaming and trumpeting as they went. That was the end of my elephant hunting on that safari.

It would almost seem that I was never meant to get one, because on subsequent trips I had no opportunity. When we went to Kenya in 1975, the issuing of elephant licenses had been suspended. In 1983 and 1997 I hunted in South Africa, where, as far as I know, there are few if any wild elephants outside the parks, and they are too intelligent and too strong to keep on fenced ranches. Also, of course, they need a lot more room than even the largest of these can provide. In 1987, even though they were overrunning and destroying forests in Botswana, there was no open season, and Zambia had long been closed to elephant hunting when I was there in 1990. Just prior to my return to Tanzania in 1993 I had intended to hunt them in one of the few places left where they can still be shot and returned to the United States legally. This is the legendary Selous Game Preserve, but I reluctantly passed it up and went to Masailand instead. Despite the fact that I thus saved myself a king's ransom in trophy fees and air charters, I am not sure but that I will always regret this decision. However, perhaps it is just as well. In any case, to this day I do not have an elephant.

Chapter 8

Things That Go Bump In the Night

In 1983 Phyllis and I went to the Republic of South Africa during the month of August. While I was there primarily for church work, there was no way in which I could fly halfway around the world to Africa without getting into the bush for at least a short hunt. So, after spending some time in the Johannesburg area, we headed into Zululand for what would be a brief 11-day safari with John Kelly as our professional. At the time he and his brother, Garry, were operating a very good safari company throughout various parts of South Africa. We started on the company's game ranch near Hluhluwe not far from St. Lucia and then we flew south to Cape Province and the Great Karroo.

South African game ranches are a good example of what intelligent reclaiming of the environment can accomplish. By the early 20th century the game was virtually gone from the Union; there had even been a deliberate attempt by Boer ranchers to exterminate all the wild animals, because they saw them as a threat to their livelihood. They almost succeeded, but not quite. A few farmers, both Boers and others of British descent, realized that they were on the verge of losing a very valuable resource. The idea of game farming, or game ranching, was born.

They first began to protect, then to raise, and finally to "sell" wild animals. The game lived under entirely natural conditions, except that the ranches, most of which were vast in size, were fenced, and because of this in desert areas, such as the Great Karroo, artificial water holes were provided. This was necessary because it was impossible for the confined game to migrate during the dry season. The experiment proved to be a great success, so great in fact that many of those men gave up farming and devoted themselves entirely to ranching of wild game. They became professional hunters and are now heavily involved in taking clients out in search of big game. This is especially true in Zululand and the Transvaal, whereas in the south many of them are still farming — often sheep farming — with game ranching as a profitable sideline. When we left Zululand and went to the Cape Province, we hunted on a 46,000-acre spread owned by Phil Van der Merwe in the Great Karroo. He had over 6,000 head of sheep on his ranch, but he also had bontebok (once on the verge of extinction), blesbok, black wildebeest (very rare in the wild), red hartebeest, both the typical and black springbok, and gemsbok — the largest of the oryx family. Clients, mostly Americans, spend a lot of money on these ranches hunting such animals, some of which, like the bontebok and white rhino, cannot legally be shot anywhere else.

No one claims that such ranch hunting even remotely resembles the old time tented safari. In the south we actually lived on Phil's ranch and ate food cooked over a kitchen range by his lovely wife, Donna. However, in Hluhluwe it bore slightly more resemblance to the old way: No houses were in evidence; we slept in thatched huts (with plumbing), had our sundowners around a campfire in the evening, and ate in a mess hut (not a tent). Once you climbed into a hunting car, there was very little difference, indeed. The animals are completely wild, and the nyala, as anyone who has hunted them on a ranch can testify, are just as shy and elusive as the truly wild ones in neighboring Mozambique. To be sure, there are fences on the South African spreads, but you rarely run across them, because the ranches are so large that the game has no more difficulty in escaping than on the veldt in East Africa. Hluhluwe is where we hunted first, and where I went after another of the spiral-horned antelopes, the nyala.

In some ways an nyala is very much like its smaller cousin, the bushbuck. It is larger, the bulls running perhaps 280 pounds, but it has many of the same habits, such as sticking to its "turf," where it can generally be found day after day. Also, while not an aquatic animal, it likes to be near water. The cows, which are hornless, are somewhat smaller and quite red in color, whereas a mature bull is dark brown — very hairy with a prominent neck mane and a long ridge of white hair running along its back — an extremely handsome animal. Like all the

1983, South Africa. Nyala are one of the main reasons that hunters flock to South Africa. Pictured above is a trophy in typical hunting country.

bushbuck family, it has striped sides and white dots on each cheek, and also has a chevron across the bridge of its nose that is common to most of the family. The big ones have "ivory-tipped" horns that, when viewed from the front, appear somewhat bell-like. They grow upward and outward and then gracefully back toward each other over the upper third of their length. As with other spiral-horned antelope, there is a double twist in the mature male, but they lack the deep curl found in greater and lesser kudu. Twenty-seven inches is certainly a respectable trophy and will get an nyala into the record book. However, in common with the whole family it is very, very difficult to get near, a most shy animal.

There were plenty of nyala on the ranch where we hunted. We saw them every day, but to find one of a trophy size and then to get within shooting range was quite another matter. The first day or two we spent most of our time in the hills where we could glass for great distances. In the course of this hunting I unexpectedly shot a bush pig. This was a bit unusual, because it is primarily a nocturnal animal and seldom seen in the light of day. I got mine only because we stumbled on a sleeping herd while struggling up a hillside on foot. In any event it provided some nice lean pork for our camp larder.

On the morning of the third day we came close. John's tracker had spotted a good bull wandering into the thickets where they spend most of their time. We went after him on foot, moving very quietly and very slowly. John got me up to within about 30 yards, and I could just make him out in the thick undergrowth. I let the safety off and raised my rifle to shoot, but at that instant, still unalarmed, he moved a bit and got a tree between us and his shoulder. When I shifted my position to get a better view, he either saw or heard us and was gone. So much for that nyala.

I was very disappointed. I remembered how hard I had worked to get my greater kudu in 1971 and how my lost opportunity on that safari had threatened to be my only chance. I assumed the same would be true with the nyala, but John assured me that we would have more opportunities. However, that had been a very superior trophy, and I might well not see one that large again. John estimated his horns at 27 inches.

We worked around the ranch all day, finding nothing worthwhile, until the sun was going down and darkness approaching (why do the bushbuck family so often seem to appear at the last gasp of daylight?). In fact, we had turned back toward camp when John spotted a lone bull quite far to our left. Of course, we stopped for a look. The only problem was that we could not see its head. It was lowered while feeding, and in addition it was hidden from our view by a bush. After what seemed forever and as the sun was sinking still lower, it finally looked up and stepped forward from behind that bush. John gulped. This was one fine nyala! Without hesitation he told me to shoot. The nyala was standing broadside to us, but it was a long shot, perhaps 250 yards in failing light. I lay prone, barely able to sight over the grass, took very deliberate aim, and touched it off. The bull whirled in a flash and disappeared into the trees behind. No one could be sure whether I had hit him or not, although the tracker thought he had

A morning visitor attracted by the smell of fresh meat emanating from camp.

heard the "thunk" of the bullet. When we got up to where he had been, sure enough, we found blood — not much, but some — and the chase was on, racing both the nyala and the gathering darkness.

At this point I should back up a little. After I shot, we left Phyllis in the hunting car with the assurance that we were just going for a look and hoped to find a dead nyala not far from where it had been standing. Even though a good sport, she was not all that keen about being left alone in an empty truck as the African sun was setting. But with a minimum of grumbling she moved into the relative safety of the cab to await our allegedly imminent return. Little did she know that would not be for quite a while and that when one is alone in Africa after dark, things do indeed go bump in the night.

For a while it was relatively easy to follow the track, but very soon the spots of blood were growing fewer and farther between. After 15 minutes or so it seemed quite evident that I had not hit him in an immediately vital spot. By then it was virtually dark, and I feared losing him entirely. John reassured me that if we had to quit because of darkness, we would come back the next day and probably find it dead. If not, we would certainly be able to track it down in the daylight. I was not very confident. My apprehension was that we would have to quit because of darkness and that the nyala would die during the night, if it were not already dead. In that case the hair might well slip before we found it the next day, and this would reduce my hypothetical trophy to a mounted skull at the very best.

It seemed at the time that we must have followed it about a half mile — in retrospect it was probably about 300 yards — but in any case the time to quit had clearly arrived. We were just about to turn back toward the car (and to what was by now a very nervous wife) when our tracker stooped and peered intently into the darkness. Then he relaxed and straightened up. About 30 yards ahead lay the beautiful nyala. My shot had gone quite low, almost missing, but it had just caught the brisket and nicked the heart. In any case the nyala was very dead. Upon subsequent measurement back in the States, he scored 28¾ inches in length, a very good nyala well up in the record book.

Because it was too dark to skin him then and there, the tracker was sent back to get Phyllis and our vehicle. After what seemed an interminable length of time, during which I was sure they were groping around in the dark, trying to locate us, we heard the welcome sound of the motor. It was not long before we could make out headlights moving slowly through the brush. As they pulled up beside us, I could see that Phyllis was driving — the first time she had ever climbed behind the wheel in the African bush! Apparently, the tracker had not known how to operate a car. This was a terrible blow to his ego — being driven by a woman. Incidentally, an amusing sequel to this occurred a few days later after I had shot an impala in John's absence (he was scouting some distance away on the other side of the hill). Once again I had had to send the tracker back to the car where Phyllis was waiting. At least, it was not after dark that time. Obviously, our tracker had been brooding over the previous incident, and he made up his mind that no matter what, he would not be humiliated again. So this time he insisted on getting behind the wheel himself. However, after struggling for some time, he simply could not shift the car into

I was lucky enough in 1983 to get this record book nyala on my first South African safari.

gear, and so there they sat. The upshot of all this was that he finally had no choice but to give up and be driven a second time — by a woman. Phyllis told me later that he started swearing in English in a manner that would make a sailor blush, but he obviously did not have the slightest idea what he was saying. Knowing no English, he was merely parroting what he had previously heard clients — and perhaps professionals — verbalize at moments of acute stress and anguish.

But to return to the nyala, after appropriate pictures by flash and under the car lights, we loaded him into the truck and started back. Then Phyllis proceeded to pour out her tale of woe. In fact, she was as mad as a boiled owl, because she felt we had abandoned her to the African night. Soon after we left, she became convinced that she heard sounds of large beasts moving about the area. She hurriedly rolled up all the windows for what dubious protection they might afford and then sat nervously, awaiting her fate, calling down all kinds of imprecations upon us for leaving her alone in the darkness. She knew that there were rhinos around, and she was certain she could hear them. I tried to reassure her that no rhino, especially no white rhino, would have assaulted her as she sat quietly in a stationary car. However, she was never convinced that we did not simply go off, leaving her at the mercy of those things that go bump in the African night.

Chapter 9

Close Encounters of the Third Kind

How dangerous is Africa? According to Hollywood one takes his life into his hands every time he — or especially she — ventures a mile out on the veldt or into the jungle. This is the popular picture we have of the "Dark Continent:" A lion crouched to charge; a leopard poised to leap from a tree onto our hero's back; hordes of crocodiles, all 15 feet long, crowding the river bank and just waiting for the unwary damsel to approach or fall into the water from one of those ubiquitous swinging bridges we used to see in the Tarzan movies. Incidentally, those bridges, always on the verge of collapse, seemed to hold out just long enough for the good guys to get across. Tarzan would then cut the vines, sending the pursuing bad guys plunging into the chasm and into the jaws of the waiting crocodiles. People still ask how I dare go to such a place.

I admit that at the time of this writing this is not quite as naive a question as it might once have seemed. There are many areas in Africa where there *is* genuine danger and where I simply would not go, no matter how tempting the game might be. In such places as Sudan, Somalia, and parts of Ethiopia, one would indeed have a great deal to fear from terrorists. Unfortunately, there is now another real threat that also keeps some people away: AIDS. However, this is a danger that is easily avoidable and it should not deter anyone from going to Africa. Nonetheless, at least parts of the "Dark Continent" can be dangerous indeed — not so much from wild beasts as from Uzis and AK-47s.

What most people are wondering about is the danger from animals. How great is this? The answer, at least based upon my *very* limited experience is: If you have plenty of insect repellent, watch where you are walking to avoid the fairly numerous, but relatively non-aggressive poisonous snakes, and if you are careful when fording rivers where there just might be a big crocodile, you can *probably* walk unarmed from Cape Town to Cairo and never be threatened by any of Africa's "fierce beasts." In fact, this very thing was done by a lone Scots woman in 1993. I am curious as to the route she took to avoid terrorists, but I can easily understand her lack of trouble from four-footed animals. Perhaps the greatest danger from a land animal would be the hippo, returning to its stretch of river in the early morning after a night of foraging. Incidentally, if you ever should try this trek, be sure to boil your drinking water along the way, because African parasites do present a *very* real danger.

Having said all this, it still cannot be denied that there is always the *possibility* of an unprovoked attack from one of the Big Five: Elephant, buffalo, rhinoceros, lion, or leopard. I say the "Big Five," but I virtually discount the last. With the exception of the *extremely* rare man-eater, unprovoked attacks by leopards are almost unknown. The only instance I have ever heard of is when Carl Akeley, the famous naturalist and father of modern American taxidermy, was jumped by a female with cubs. Fortunately, she was a small one and he managed to throttle her bare-handed. Incidentally, it is my understanding that when he used to tell this story, he invariably omitted a very significant point: The leopard tried to take him as he was relieving himself in the bushes. This fact probably saved his life. He was squatting, and his shins thus protected his abdomen and prevented it from being ripped open by the dying leopard's hind feet as she desperately struggled to escape his grip.

However, it has to be admitted that the other four are a threat — a minimal one, to be sure, but a threat nonetheless. Later on I will discuss the most dangerous game from the perspective of hunting, but right now I am talking about *casual* danger and a few occasions when things got a bit close for me in chance encounters with animals I was not specifically hunting. Only once have I had to shoot something in self-defense under such circumstances: That was when I finished off a buffalo that Dave had first dropped in an unprovoked and totally unexpected charge. In addition to this one experience there have been a few other interesting incidents. One or two scared me a bit, and

A white rhinoceros on a South African game ranch (1983).

several had a downright humorous aspect to them.

I have never hunted rhino. I got there just too late. They could still be taken legally in 1971 when I hunted in Tanzania, but they were already getting very scarce, and I had no desire at that time to hasten them toward what even then looked like inevitable extinction. I saw several on that and subsequent safaris, and we did have one unexpected run-in. Dave Ommanney, my two sons, and I were tracking a zebra which I had wounded, when a rhino suddenly burst out of nowhere. It was about 70 yards away and immediately started toward us on the run. I did not have a rhino license, so I wanted to avoid at all costs (save that of being gored) having to shoot the poor fellow. Also, any attempt on my part would almost certainly have been futile, because my .270 was loaded with soft points, and that is hardly an ideal rifle or cartridge for stopping a charging rhino. So when it loomed large in front of us, I quickly handed the rifle to Dave with the urgent suggestion, "Here, you shoot him; I don't want to." He did not either, so all four of us, plus the trackers, took off for the dubious shelter of the safari car a couple of hundred yards away. The rhino must have lost sight of us, or lost interest, because it soon quit; on the other hand maybe it simply thought it had carried the day, which indeed it had. In any case, I am proud to say that even though I was the oldest in flight, I beat them all to the truck!

Over the years I have had several interesting run-ins with buffalo. I have already alluded to one. I always worry a little about *mbogo* when I go off alone after francolin with only a 12-gauge shotgun loaded with 7½s. In fact, I unashamedly admit to being *afraid* of these wild bovines. I have shot enough of them so that every time Dave would say we needed another one for bait, I would begin to breathe nervously. Twice I have been charged by them and, thanks to Dave Ommanney, have twice escaped unscathed. Now I fear that the law of averages may be catching up with me. Although I certainly respect them all, I am not especially nervous with other dangerous game, but buffalo give me chilblains. Thus when bird shooting, I am nervous about simply startling an old bull sleeping in the brush. He might well decide to come for me rather than run, in which case with only the armament at hand I would find myself seriously under gunned. I have never had any trouble while bird shooting, but one interesting and somewhat amusing buffalo incident in which I was an observer comes to mind.

In 1975 my wife and I were on safari in Kenya with our good friends, Ralph and Gunlog Millet, from Connecticut. Dave Ommanney was again the professional. One morning we were in the two safari cars, looking for whatever we might find. Presently, we stopped by a small swamp — or a large mud hole, whichever you prefer — to have a hot cup of tea (an essential routine in a Britisher's day). Ralph decided to answer a call of nature behind a large tree over near the swamp (how often the unexpected happens at such times), and Solomon, our Kamba professional trainee, had casually ambled down to the mud hole to have a look around. Then everything seemed to happen at once: A bull buffalo that had been slumbering peacefully in the mud awoke with a start and exploded out of it. A somewhat pallid Solomon charged back toward the car, and Ralph emerged hurriedly from behind the tree — his face also now several shades paler. No harm was

Cottar's lions relaxing near camp (Masai Mara, 1975).

done, because the buff had elected to flee, but it could well have been otherwise. Needless to say, I was convulsed with laughter. Of course, I happened to be standing safely by the car at the critical moment.

I had a similar experience on the same safari when Dave and I were hunting at about 8,000 feet in the Loita Hills. Incidentally, it was there that I had my first encounter with poison nettles. I strongly recommend that one avoid skin contact with this insidious plant. Some time after that unpleasant experience one of the trackers stopped dead in his tracks and pointed into some thick brush about 10 feet in front. I could see nothing, and certainly had not heard a sound, but somehow he communicated to Dave that there was a buffalo standing there. Dave raised his rifle and told me to do the same. Then there was a crash as the bull broke and fled. Again, he could just as easily have come for us; in fact Dave admitted that he was a little surprised that he had not charged. That would have been diverting, indeed.

I will relate one more buffalo incident before moving on to the cats. This one, however, was not entirely spontaneous, because we were hunting them at the time and thus to some extent, brought it on ourselves.

I was still trying to improve on a bull I had shot earlier in that same 1975 safari. One afternoon we stopped the two cars to glass a herd grazing in the open some distance away. It was obvious that we could not see all the buffalo, many of them being hidden behind a little knoll that projected out from the right. Ralph, Dave, and I started across — Dave with his .470 and I with the .375. We asked Ralph, who was not hunting buffalo, whether he wanted to come along to see what happened. He allowed that he would, but as events turned out he must shortly have felt awfully naked, because he was wholly unarmed.

We had no trouble walking up on the fairly large herd. They watched us coming, but were unalarmed, probably because the wind was in our favor, and they could not get our scent. Presently, we were right in among them, and still they did not run. Instead they fanned out a bit and formed an arc that extended across to our right and left. At this point I had grown definitely uncomfortable, and I remember looking back over my shoulder and seeing a rather sickly grin on Ralph's face — certainly, not a happy look, but one that must have reflected my own. At the same time I was trying to signal Dave that perhaps we were close enough. Either he did not hear me, or he simply pretended not to hear. In any case we kept on going, drawing even closer. Anyone who has ever gotten really close to a big buff knows what I mean when I say that as it looks at you, that malevolent expression on its face seems to say "You owe me money!" This was just the way these fellows glared at us. Then they could stand it no longer and fright took over. They broke and ran some distance to our left. Dave had not spotted any particularly good heads among them, so we let them go — assuming we had seen the last of them.

Instead of retracing our original route, which had necessitated wading through some pretty wet and swampy ground, we continued around the knoll, hoping to find a drier way back to the cars and some rather anxious wives, who had been watching everything. Then the unexpected happened: As we came around the hill, we almost ran over

Tasty?

two young bulls that had become separated from the herd. We stopped; they stopped. From a distance of 10-15 yards we stared at each other in amazement. When one of them took a couple of tentative steps toward us, it was tense, and Dave and I both started to raise our rifles. But then, instead, he simply took off his cap and waved it at them, shouting, "Bug off!" At this they whirled, described a wide berth around us and chased after the rest of the herd. You could almost hear them yelling, "Hey, fellas, wait for us!" Ralph and I wiped the sweat from our brows.

When we were safely back in the cars, I protested warmly that our extremely close proximity to the herd had been just a bit much. Dave laughed and assured us that a *herd* of buffalo almost never makes trouble, and they had not. They had simply stood there, looking at us like so many cattle in a pasture until it had become too much for them, and they had had to run. However, the two bulls we subsequently surprised as we were heading back to the car; that could have been a different story.

In the movies, with the possible exception of the Great White Hunter, the lion is most often depicted as chasing the heroine. Yet in my own experience, while I once had a very frightening experience with one I had wounded, I cannot say that I have ever been seriously threatened by any lions that I was not hunting. However, three instances do come to mind which could have been serious if the lions had wanted to make them so, but they did not, and two of these were over almost as soon as they started.

In 1987 John Northcote and I were hunting along the Chobe River for red lechwe and sitatunga. We had just driven down from the track on to the riverbank itself, when I asked him to stop for a moment to let me step next to a bush. He dutifully complied, and I casually strolled a few feet away in front of some brush. Normally at such times the others find occasion to search for game, looking in the opposite direction. But this time John was frantically trying to attract my attention for some reason — for some *very* urgent reason. I did not understand, but then something caught my eye: In the thick brush not 12 *feet* in front, I saw the yellow eyes of a lioness quietly watching me. It does not take much imagination to guess what I did next.

I cannot imagine why she had let me get that close without either running away or jumping me. I can only guess that because there had been no eye contact, she knew I had not spotted her, and so was lying low. Then when our eyes finally did meet, I reacted so quickly in the opposite direction that she knew I was no threat to her and just stayed where she was. She was watching serenely as we drove off and was still there when we returned that way an hour or so later. I did not ask John to stop the second time.

Another unexpected brush I had with lions was on our 1975 trip to Kenya. It was mid-afternoon and late in the safari. I had already gotten most of what I had come for, so Dave and I were casually strolling along the edge of some woods with no serious hunting in mind. I was still looking for that big buffalo (that I never did get), but the safari was winding down. I knew Dave did not expect anything much, because he was not carrying his rifle; instead he had some paperback thriller stuffed in his pocket and was obviously looking forward to a bit of relaxation with his pipe and book while we still-hunted until dusk.

We were ambling along without a care in the world. Dave was in front, followed by me and then the gun bearers. We were approaching a curve in the path, and because there was fairly thick brush on both sides, could not see what was around the turn. Suddenly, Dave stopped short and then almost knocked me over as he charged by me in an effort to reach the tracker, who was carrying his rifle. I had heard a "woof" as he turned and had looked up to see a half-grown lion cub, racing off into the brush to our right. Apparently Dave had seen more than that. As he came around the bend, right in front of him and only a few feet away were two lionesses *with a cub*, and one of them and Dave were just about to walk over each other. It is difficult to say who was more surprised. They were so nonplussed that the lions did not even growl. One of them uttered one "woof" and they leapt away. The cub, which I had seen, went in another direction — as did Dave.

In all the time I have spent in the African bush with this great professional, this is the only time I ever saw Dave Ommanney even come close to losing his *veddy, veddy* British cool in the presence of game.

On my 1993 safari he and I had another somewhat startling encounter with lions. I shot a buffalo late one afternoon, and because it was getting dark, we simply covered it with some thorn bushes and returned to camp.

Upon our return the next morning to retrieve it for lion bait, we discovered someone had beaten us to the punch. The buffalo had been cleared of thorn bushes and worked over by a lion or lions during the night. As we piled out of the car, we heard a very deep and unmistakably menacing growl, telling us, "Watch out." We did. At that point a lioness and a cub jumped up and fled. They had been watching us from some nearby bushes as we were approaching and then had growled a warning when we got out of the car. Mama obviously felt we had gotten just a bit too close for comfort. However, when we saw the lioness and her cub run, we relaxed, and Dave and the trackers started to examine the ground around the dead buffalo to see whether there had also been a good male at work the night before. Then we heard still another deep and even more persistent growl. Dave spoke up and told me in no uncertain terms to stop wandering around in such a casual manner, armed only with my video camera. This admonition was enough for me, and I sidled quickly over to the open door of our hunting car. It seems it was enough for the cause of our alarm as well, because another lioness then jumped up and fled. Apparently, this was Auntie who had stayed behind to make sure we did not make any trouble with the mother and cub. None of them had cared for our messing around with their free meal.

It is somewhat ironic that when one stalks a lion bait in the predawn, it must be done without even snapping a twig, or any lion on the bait will be gone. In this case, however, several of us were wandering around right out in the open, talking like a bunch of magpies, and the two lionesses hung around and were warning us but were obviously not very alarmed. Perhaps this was because they sensed that we were not hunting them, whereas the snap of a twig at dawn is an unmistakable sound of danger. Speaking of cats, apart from the leopard I shot with John Northcote in 1987, I had only one encounter with those beautiful animals and that was on a 1975 safari in Kenya. Dave and I had been working very hard to get a big lion and we had hung baits in several promising places. But apart from one lioness and a couple of hyenas nothing had been working on them. Then one day our hopes for success got a real boost, because we discovered that a good male had been feeding on one of the baits. We knew this because we found long hairs from a lion's mane caught on the bark of the tree from which the wildebeest was hanging. This was very encouraging, even exciting, because we had begun to think that all the big lions had gotten smart and gone into the parks.

Dave and the trackers then set about building an approach and a blind overlooking the bait. Unless one is going to spend a night in a machan (a thrilling experience, I might add), the building of an approach is an art and must be done very carefully, or there will be little chance of getting close enough for a shot. The car should be left no nearer than half a mile away, because the sound of an engine carries a great distance in the early morning. The approach itself must not be visible from the bait. A deep ditch or gully is ideal, except that they usually have lots of noisy dead leaves in them. The alternative is to crawl over open ground, in which case trees and bushes along the way help. If the plan is to go to a bait this way, the first job is to lay out an approach route and then build a large and high blind no more than 50 yards from the bait. Incidentally, when the approach route has been completed, it is very helpful to hang toilet paper on the bushes along the way; otherwise, it is easy to get off it in the early morning darkness.

There is nothing quite as exciting as checking lion bait. In the half-light of dawn you crawl slowly — usually painfully — over the ground, trying to avoid all noise and always keeping the blind between you and the bait. When you finally arrive, you usually do not know what if anything is there. So you stand up very slowly and peer through the small peephole.

Sometimes, in fact usually, the bait will be untouched. If lions have been there during the night, they have often left before you arrive. Occasionally, you find a hyena or two feeding, in which case you *know* no lions are about. But every now and then everything works, and you discover a lion on the bait, or more likely several of them lying around it. If they are actually feeding, you may well know it even before getting there, because they often squabble over food with grunts and growls. I have never actually made a successful stalk and found a good male on the bait. Once we did discover a young male and a couple of lionesses on one, and on another occasion, after spending a night in a machan, we awoke to watch two immature males feeding. That was quite a thrill, even though they were too young and scruffy to be considered trophies. But, I have yet to see a big fellow come to bait.

However, on those rare occasions when everything works out as it is meant to, after looking a pride over, you will usually see His Majesty lying to one side, sleeping off a gigantic meal of wildebeest, zebra, buffalo, hippo, or whatever bait you may have been using. Then you have your chance, *and don't muff it.*

This morning we got up before daylight to check the bait. Ironically, as we were driving, huddled in the predawn cold, a very nice lion raced across the track in front of our headlights, only to disappear immediately in the darkness. When we finally arrived at the beginning of the approach, we killed the engine, moved stiffly out of the car and started to crawl. By the time we reached the blind, it was light enough to see our sights, and Dave rose very slowly to look through the peephole while I held my breath in anticipation. Regrettably, from the way he relaxed and turned to me, I knew right away that nothing was there. So we casually walked out and went over to see whether anything had been there during the night.

Suddenly, our tracker stopped and clicked his tongue. They often use this signal to attract the professional's attention. I had neither seen nor heard anything, but wc all stood absolutely still, listening and looking around. Then I did notice a sound — one that is hard to describe — something like a growl or a snarl, but not quite. Obviously, there was a large cat somewhere *very* near by. Everyone was puzzled, because it did not sound exactly like a lion, and why would one be growling at us anyhow, unless it was a lioness with a cub? Usually, they simply run off without a sound. Whatever it was, it kept on, and then it dawned on us that it was not growling at *us* at all, but at something or someone else. With our rifles ready, we worked *very* carefully and *very* quietly into the brush from which the strange sounds seemed to be coming. They kept on and on, but did not quite seem to be angry growls, yet they were frequent and loud.

After some prolonged and cautious creeping, I saw the tracker suddenly laugh silently and whisper something to Dave, who then began an equally silent retreat. When we had gotten out of earshot, I asked, "What was going on in there? What was it?" Dave laughed and said that it was a pair of leopards making love. We had never actually seen them, but must have gotten to within a few yards of where

Time to surrender the right of way (Kenya, 1975).

they were carrying on. Only under such circumstances as these would it *ever* be possible to get as close to leopards as we had. Then I realized what that strange noise had been. It was not all that different from what our female cat at home used to make when she was in a similar state — it was *caterwauling*. Since I was not after leopard on that safari and did not have a license for one anyhow, we did not disturb them and considerately crept away, leaving them in their connubial bliss. May their tribe ever increase.

Then there are elephants. Normally these huge pachyderms lead a pretty much live-and-let-live existence. Occasionally, you hear of a rogue that makes trouble and has to be killed, but they usually leave you well enough alone if you do the same with them. If you are in the protected game preserves where they are relatively tame, avoid getting between a cow and her calf, and you will probably have no trouble.

But we were not in the game parks, and we could not leave well enough alone. One day Ralph Millet and I were with Dave in his hunting car when we spotted a fair-sized herd of cows and calves. This was 1975 in Kenya after elephant hunting had been closed, so we were interested only in photography. Dave asked whether we would like to take pictures of a charge. On my first safari I obtained spectacular results when we had done this with a cow and calf rhino on the Serengeti. Ralph and I were both very enthusiastic. He climbed into the back of the truck and got his camera all set for the pictures of a lifetime — charging elephants. As we approached them, it was interesting to see how the cows herded the youngsters into the center and formed a protective ring about them. Elephants are very family oriented animals. Then as we drew still nearer, the herd's matriarch began to make threatening gestures and mock charges. Fearlessly, if not foolishly, we pressed on. Suddenly, it was no longer a question of *mock* charges. The old girl, trumpeting with rage, came right for us, with Ralph clicking away from the open truck bed. Dave gunned the motor and we had no trouble staying safely in front of her. Finally, she let out one more scream and seemed to quit — probably in a spirit of triumph. We thought it over for the moment and stopped some distance away to let Ralph put a new roll of film into his camera. When we suddenly heard some frantic banging on the cab's roof, we looked out and saw the cow coming like an express train — and not far away. With some rapid acceleration and grinding of gears, we were again able to outdistance her, but I swear Ralph must have almost felt her hot breath on him. Dave insisted that it had all been bluff and that no harm had been intended. She would *never* have plucked Ralph from the truck, but try to convince him of that.

We had another run-in with elephants on the same safari. Again, we were out cruising, this time in both hunting cars. Presently, Dave spotted three bulls, perhaps 300 yards away, and one of these appeared to have pretty fair ivory.

Remember that elephant hunting had been closed in Kenya in 1975. This is not quite true. The *issuing of elephant licenses* had been suspended, but if anyone had an unfilled one, dated prior to the suspension, it was still valid. Dave, who had never shot an elephant to collect tusks for himself, had such a license and thought he might fill it now.

What a curl.

He, Ralph, and I started to stalk the three bulls. However, after a 100 yards or so Ralph, who was having trouble with his legs, decided to stop and watch what we would do. The wind was right, and the elephants were preoccupied with stripping thorn trees, so we were able to get quite close. I could not believe that we could just keep walking right up to them without being seen, but on we went with my heart beating faster by the moment.

By now I think Dave had made up his mind that he would not shoot any of them, if he had *ever* really so intended (something I doubt in light of later events in the safari). The largest probably carried about 50-55 pounds per tusk. This is about the best one might expect today, but not in 1975. Anyhow, for whatever reason, he decided against shooting any of them, but his professionalism drove him to get just as close as possible. Then suddenly, and without warning, they turned and came right toward us. I almost had cardiac arrest, but Dave seemed unalarmed. Stooping low, he sidled quickly to his right — with me right behind. I did not see how we could possibly get out unscathed without shooting at least one of the elephants, but we kept moving to the right until presently they rushed by us only a few yards away and were gone. As I turned to watch them go, I happened to glance back and noticed Ralph just preparing to climb a tree a couple of hundred yards behind us; he has always denied this as a gross calumny.

During the postmortem of this adventure I was incredulous. I simply could not believe that the elephants had not been charging, but Dave said they had never seen us and throughout the whole episode were totally oblivious of our presence. What had happened was that a herd of zebra 100 yards or so beyond them *had* seen us and were barking and running in alarm. In the excitement of stalking the elephants, I had not even noticed them, but the elephants had, and when the zebra became frightened and fled, the elephants did the same thing, albeit in the opposite direction — right toward us. Apparently they were unconscious of the fact that the source of all this excitement was practically underfoot.

As a postscript I might add that Dave never did get his elephant. He tried once more a little later in the same safari, actually getting up to within a few yards of a slowly moving mixed herd in which there was a pretty fair bull. Dave had his eye on that one, but when he was about to brain it, the bull lifted his trunk and draped it over a calf walking beside it. This hard-boiled professional never fired the shot; instead he turned and quietly walked back to us. His only comment was, "I just couldn't do it."

Chapter 10

African Aerobics: Shake, Rattle and Roll

On four safaris I was accompanied by my long-suffering but loyal wife, Phyllis. The first time she came was in 1975, when we went to Kenya with two good friends from Connecticut. That was fine, because it was new and novel. In 1983 we went to Zululand and the Great Karroo in South Africa. This was not too bad either, because we had first toured some of the game parks in Kenya with our Bishop and his wife, also from Connecticut (who then went on their own way). We subsequently had an interesting two weeks near Johannesburg while I worked in a local parish. But most important from her perspective, the subsequent hunting part of the safari was mercifully brief — only 11 days. However, the junkets began to get tedious for Phyllis in 1987, when we took a 28-day trip in Botswana. The heat and, above all, the drought-produced dust were appalling, and even the company of still another good friend from Connecticut could not alleviate the pain of incredibly rough driving and the boredom of what by then Phyllis considered a rather unrelenting diet, very high in protein. When I decided to go to Zambia in 1990, there were quite a few remonstrances — in fact, howls of anguish — but when she realized we would be taking our oldest grandson, she did relent. She drew the line in 1993. Here are some of *her* impressions of the glories of safari life, written two years before her death.

"My memories of African safaris are not so much of magnificent animals or breathtaking sunsets as of a series of vehicles, including small airplanes (which occasionally wandered off course), bouncing safari cars, dugout canoes and unstable boats in crocodile and malaria infested swamps, and hot air balloons. Africa is a huge continent, and distances between cities as well as hunting areas are long. Imagine

Oh, those elephant tracks left over from the rainy season. They can cause problems.

arising at 4:30 a.m. in the pitch dark, driving three hours in a Land Rover to check a very smelly bait hung in a tree in hopes that a lion would want a dead hippo for his breakfast. Needless to say, after the first safari I would put my head under the pillow and sleep until the mighty hunters returned for breakfast at a more sensible hour. Somehow they never understood my reluctance to join them on their predawn excursions.

Clearing the track of elephant destruction. Henry supervises the "engineers."

"Frankly, I never saw any of Hank's trophies from the time he aimed his rifle until they were brought into our house and actually hung on the wall. Some of the people who accompanied us on safari were fascinated by the skinning and salting process. Not I.

"On our trip to Zambia in 1990 we made 15 — yes, 15 — different airplane flights, most of them by small charter. You can well imagine that it is rather disconcerting to be flying over vast forested areas, dotted with small lakes and streams, only to have the pilot turn to you and say that he seemed to have lost the airstrip. Granted that airstrips in Africa are generally nothing more than wide dusty openings between trees. Nevertheless, most of them have windsocks and perhaps a strip of whitewash with an arrow to indicate their existence. Obviously, we did finally land safely.

"Safari cars are not built for comfort, but are well supplied with roll bars as well as posts that can be used for support when the driver takes off across the rock-hard plains. Sometimes it seems that drivers wholly disregard the various foot-deep holes made by elephants during the rainy season as they wandered through what had then been mud. I prefer to stand and bend my knees as we hit the bumps. On one occasion Hank had the misfortune to be thrown off the high seat on to the roll bar when the Toyota Land Cruiser in which he was riding suddenly crashed into a large and unseen pit hidden in the high grass. As this was only the third day of the safari, there was no way he was going to return to Lusaka to see a doctor. Safaris come first. It was discovered later that he had probably badly bruised some ribs and crushed his sternum.

"As Hank already mentioned, I have driven a Land Cruiser twice — both times in Zululand. In the first instance he, the guide, and the tracker abandoned me in the car to track an nyala that Hank had hit. As darkness fell, I was still waiting in the open car for their return. Because I am basically a coward, I imagined that every sound I heard was an animal waiting to pounce on me. Suddenly, out of the night appeared the tracker, who indicated that I should drive the Land Cruiser while he directed me. As the steering wheel was on the right, everything had to be done in an opposite manner from which I was accustomed, and I managed to stall out a few times. Even though my Zulu was worse than his English, by gesture and sound, over hill and through brush we finally reached Hank and the guide with the now very dead nyala. I carefully did not look as they placed it in the back of the truck.

"Never expecting a repeat performance, the next day we went after an impala. Again, they dashed off after the animal, but this time it was

Luckily this was not our car. How this tourist vehicle got so far into the lake at Ngorongoro is anyone's guess. (We dragged it out.)

not dark. Again the tracker returned, but instead of letting me drive, to avoid further damage to his ego, he attempted it himself. Someone neglected to tell him that the clutch was there for a purpose, and as he struggled to get it into gear, the air became blue with oaths in English that he must have learned from American clients. However, it soon became clear even to him that he was not going to move that car, so he most reluctantly let me take over.

"On one of our trips to Kenya we drove to the Masai Mara over 90 miles of desperately rutted, pothole-filled, dusty roads. Fortunately, we returned to Nairobi by airplane — an old DC-3, which picked us up after landing on a grass runway from which zebras and various antelopes had first been chased. Travel brochures extol the beauty of East Africa (which is certainly true), but the dust is overlooked, unless you realize that the tan of the safari clothes has a real purpose: To hide the dust.

This pile up almost broke some of my ribs. I was thrown on to the gun rack. Concealed potholes are a real threat.

"The most terrifying means of transportation for me was a hot air balloon ride over the Mara during the wildebeest migration. Our friend, Tami Miglio — a veteran at balloon travel, having taken a flight in Connecticut — assured me that I'd love it. We were awakened at 4:30 a.m. (in Africa *everything* seems to start at 4:30 in the morning), and as we stumbled in the dark to the waiting van we were nearly trampled by a herd of galloping zebras. Next, when we arrived at the departure site, it was necessary to sign an accident waiver before we could leave. The balloon was spread out, filled with air, and then the command was given to get into the basket, lie on your back, and hold on. At this point, I said to Hank, "This is not my idea of fun." He tried to reassure me. As I had no choice, up we went. What frankly surprised (and terrified) me was the noise and the heat of the gas jets. But in between these spurts of gas, it was absolutely quiet, and we drifted over the wildebeest in their seemingly endless march to the north. Sometimes from an altitude of 1,000 feet, sometimes from only 10 feet, we could see wildebeest and zebra with lions watching for stragglers in the hopes of an early breakfast. Because of wayward winds we somehow drifted away from the Land Rovers, which were meant to be following us with a champagne breakfast. Consequently, there was a delay of about an hour after we landed in the midst of the wildebeest (and lions) before we enjoyed the fancy repast.

"The 1990 trip to Kenya and Zambia was probably my last, and the company of our grandson, Charles Umiker, made it very special for both Hank and me. Although we were concerned that he would be bored, Charles never let on — if indeed he was. Children of the native villages learned his name (which they pronounced 'Chawuz') and greeted him with wild enthusiasm as we would from time to time ride through their villages in our open safari cars. Charles always waved graciously, as Queen Elizabeth might do under similar circumstances. One night we had a very tough kudu stew, but he endured this without complaint. A further torment: Tsetse flies were everywhere at our last camp, so he and I were even reduced to playing cards under our mosquito netting to get away from them. Through it all he was a good sport.

"One redeeming and final example of our travel experiences: On the way home we flew from Amsterdam to Boston in Business Class with four attendants for 12 of us in that section. We were offered champagne before we even sat down and then ate our way across the Atlantic. *That* is my idea of the right way to go!"

Chapter 11

Ship Ahoy!

One of the strangest African antelopes is also one of the most rarely seen: The sitatunga. It is another of the spiral-horned family, and at first glance it resembles the nyala. However, its horns, while similar, usually do not quite complete the second curl, and the upper third flares outward rather than turning back as with the nyala. Its habits and habitat are entirely different. The sitatunga is a beautifully adapted aquatic mammal and is completely at home in the swamps, but resembles the proverbial fish out of water when forced on to dry ground. The sitatunga's hoofs are splayed and greatly elongated. Consequently, it moves easily over bogs, but the hooves hold it to a virtual and labored walk on dry land. In fact, it is so at home in the water that it often will not flee when alarmed, but simply submerge, leaving only its nostrils above the surface.

The habitat of the sitatunga's various subspecies ranges over much of Africa, from the West Coast across Zaire to the Victoria *Nyanza* and down the Nile into Sudan, south into Zambia, Tanzania, and Botswana, finally turning west again into Angola. They live in the papyrus swamps and for one very simple reason are rarely hunted successfully — relatively speaking: It is very difficult to see an animal four feet tall in papyrus that is 10 feet high. Sometimes a sitatunga can be spotted from a blind in a tree, but in Botswana when the hunter is successful, more often than not he shoots from a boat.

My introduction to this antelope took place in Botswana in 1987, and was bizarre to say the least. In fact, it was nearly calamitous. Late in the safari, after quite successful hunting our attentions turned seriously to sitatunga. Previously we had halfheartedly driven along the riverbank and even sat for periods of time in trees overlooking the papyrus, but this did not produce what I was after. I did manage to get a nice red lechwe this way, but we saw no male sitatunga. Then a boat became available to us — and what a boat!

A lot could be written about the saga of that vessel. The aluminum hull was sound, except that its bow and stern flotation tanks could not be closed, so they were completely useless in the event of capsizing. If that happened, the boat would simply plunge to the bottom of the river. A previous safari had jerry-built a superstructure on which the professional and client could sit in comfort and look over the papyrus in search of prey. The only problem was that there were no outriggers or pontoons on the boat. Consequently, it had stability something akin to a birch bark canoe shooting the Colorado River through the Grand Canyon.

The clients from that safari were from Germany, and one of them, a woman of very ample proportions, had clambered up the superstructure and ensconced herself ready to shoot the first sitatunga that stirred. The trouble was that as they were proceeding out into the river, she moved, and the boat went over. Apparently, she was running before she hit the water — for fear of crocodiles (and there were plenty around). Fortunately, everyone made it safely to shore, but the boat, motor, and rifles all went to the bottom. Naturally, it fell to the professional to recover same. After he had made several surface dives into the murky waters, trying not to think of unseen saurian companions lurking nearby, the boat was eventually secured and dragged ashore. Everything was recovered. Apparently even the rifles were all right, but that was the end of their sitatunga hunting.

Well, to be forewarned is to be forearmed, so when we decided to risk it ourselves, we did so with great care. By then the motor had been dried out and was running again, so late one afternoon we launched the boat in the hope that we would not go down like the *Titanic*. All went well on the way out; we even saw a male sitatunga — too small to shoot, however. As it began to get dark and very cold we turned back toward our home port. Dave Ommanney and I were in the superstructure, and John Northcote, the old Royal Navy veteran of the Narvik campaign, was tending the outboard motor. Suddenly, for some unexplained reason the throttle stuck and we took off like one of those great power-boats in the Gold Cup race. Dave and I hung

1987, Botswana. The author poses with his blue wildebeest.

on as best we could as we saw the hull keel over alarmingly. John struggled with the throttle, and we watched helplessly as freeboard was reduced to an inch or two above the foaming water on the starboard side. Then just as we were resigning ourselves to a swim, John got the motor under control and the crisis was over; the whole episode had only taken a few seconds, but it had been alarming indeed. We subsequently cruised back to our launching spot very slowly indeed and thought no more about sitatunga that afternoon.

If we had capsized, it really could have been serious. At the climactic moment we were probably a half a mile from shore and would certainly have had to swim for it. I really am apprehensive about what might have happened in that event — with some very large crocs living in those waters. I suppose we would have made it, but still do not like to think about it. In any case we got back shaken, but dry and unscathed.

The next day we tried again, quite halfheartedly and *very* carefully, but again without success. However, not long afterwards the company got a truck out to us with a pair of very battered and leaky pontoons. After a lot of trial and error John and Dave finally got them secured to the outriggers with the help of Peter Hepburn, one of the company's young professionals, who was in camp on a busman's holiday with his wife and small son. I was serving as supervising engineer. The sea trials then took place and were passed with flying colors. The boat was as steady as the *Queen Mary*. To be sure, one pontoon soon filled with water, but although this slowed us down considerably and gave us a bit of a list, it did not reduce our stability.

So with a minimum of trepidation we decided to have another go at finding sitatunga. This time, however, and for the next several days thereafter, it was abnormally cold and very windy. Consequently, they were lying low; absolutely nothing was moving in the swamp. To continue would simply be a waste of time, so we reluctantly decided to call it off until the gale had died down, and it had warmed up a bit.

A couple of days later, things finally began to go our way; it was not as warm as we would have liked, but at least the air was calming down. We determined to go to the river that evening, and after casting apprehensive eyes on our craft, even my wife Phyllis and our friend Tami Miglio joined us.

With our boat problems behind and the weather at least passable, our job now was to find a trophy sitatunga. So far we had seen only females and one or two immature males — nothing shootable. We traveled a mile or so into the swamp and landed on an island near the main channel of the river itself. Placing ourselves strategically in order

Also taken on this same safari near the Chobe River was a red lechwe.

to see as close to 360 degrees around us as possible, we sat down to look and wait.

As a rule I enjoy still-hunting — sitting and watching for something to appear. However, I have had remarkably little personal success with it, even though I had gotten my first greater kudu this way and once or twice I have had deer appear. Also, as we shall see, the high point of this safari would prove to be the result of long and patient waiting. But even though still-hunting has produced relatively little for me, I like it for two reasons: First, I am essentially lazy and like to sit; and second, when successful, it means that the hunter has arranged to shoot under conditions of his choosing, rather than the animal's. When it is on the animal's terms, it almost always forces one to hurry a shot, work around a bush, or, worst of all, walk to the ends of the earth. But it is so easy just to pick a nice comfortable spot, sit down, and imagine the animal walking out into plain view, totally unaware of your presence and just waiting to be shot. The only trouble is that for me, at least, the animal seldom cooperates, and this evening was no exception.

When we were within an hour or so of sunset, we gave up and started to work our way back, slowly motoring up various byways hoping to see a good male if and when one at last came out to feed after the long spell of cold weather. Once again Dave and I were aloft with John at the helm; the girls were huddled in the cold up forward. As the light was beginning to fade, as it always seems to be the case, Dave spotted a fairly good male feeding in the papyrus. He was over 350 yards away — much too far for a shot from a moving boat in failing light, so John throttled down and started working us into shooting range as quietly as possible. Finally, getting as close as he dared, he grounded us on a bog, leaving me with a shot of about 230 yards over the papyrus tops. This would still be a pretty long one under the circumstances, but I had no choice. It was impossible to stalk the animal, because he would surely hear us slogging through the swamp long before we could get close enough for a shot over the papyrus reeds. I found out later that there is some risk in walking on those floating bogs. It is possible to break through and go to the bottom of the river — crisis time indeed — as one then has to grope his way up through the muddy water, trying to find the opening before he drowns.

Actually, although it was a fairly long shot from the boat, another factor made it somewhat easier: When hunting this way, the client is seated in a comfortable chair with a railing on which to rest as he aims. The upshot was that I hit the sitatunga on my first shot. However, he did not go down, and Dave hurriedly told me to shoot again. I did, and he dropped. Now I had my sitatunga, but he still had to be retrieved.

Typical of the way we hunted the Chobe River area for sitatunga (after the pontoons were installed).

Our trackers had gone on strike. Because John had not brought them lunch earlier in the day, they refused to go out with us that afternoon (this would *never* have happened on the long-gone old-time safaris in of East Africa). So we set off without them. This meant that if my sitatunga were to be recovered, *we* would have to do it. In this case "we" meant Dave and John. They clambered out of the boat and plodded across the bog up to their knees in water. When they finally reached it and had tied a short rope around its horns, the long haul started — amidst terrible groans, grunts, and expostulations from two aging professionals. Phyllis and Tami were sure they would have heart attacks and were berating me for not going out to lend a hand. Never wondering whether *I* might have a heart attack if I ventured forth. In my own defense, I had twice offered to do so, but the pros had said they could handle it — at which point I did not press the issue. I happened to be dry and relatively warm, and I could see no reason for another of us (namely me) getting wet and miserable and perhaps even running the risk of pneumonia — especially at the prices I was paying said professionals, who, of course, love every aspect of their work. However, I did throw them a line when they got to within 30 feet of the boat. They tied it around the animal's horns, and, hauling from the boat, I was able to help a bit, getting it in over the last few yards. However, because of all this a bit of my macho image had worn off in the eyes of my female companions, and I got the silent treatment for a while — at least until after the first round of drinks around the campfire. In any case, my manhood did not suffer nearly as much as that of the striking trackers. In the eyes of their peers they were disgraced, because the white *bwanas* had gone out, shot, and then brought back a trophy sitatunga without them. We heard through the grapevine that their lives were made pretty miserable that evening, and I am happy to report that there were no further strikes.

My sitatunga, while not making Rowland Ward's record book is, nonetheless, a perfectly respectable male. One cannot be too choosy on the first one, because they are not that easy to come by. All in all, I was most happy, having survived the perils of the deep and also having added still another spiral-horned antelope to my trophy room wall.

Chapter 12

A Cold Morning In the Swamp

In 1990 I returned to south central Africa, this time to Zambia — again with my guide of many years, David Ommanney. My wife, Phyllis, and Tami Miglio came again. This time we had a very important fourth member: our oldest grandchild, Charles Umiker, aged nine. Starting with my father in 1913, Charles represents the fourth generation in our family to go on an African safari, and although he did no hunting, Dave introduced him to target shooting with a .22. Who knows whether he may yet return to drink again of the waters of Africa and this time with a rifle?

Zambia is a sad example of how bad game management and very lax policing of poachers can virtually destroy a hunter's paradise. The famous Luangwa Valley, teeming with game only 10 years earlier, had been hammered to the point where there was little left. This was due partly to the bad game management, as well as to the irresponsible use of hunting concessions by some safari companies. However, even more devastating has been the appalling meat poaching that is almost universal in a country where the native population is literally starving to death. It is difficult to blame these people who are shooting, snaring and trapping animals illegally in order to feed their families. Under the circumstances one can not feel too much bitterness toward them, but what will happen when the game is gone, which will soon be the case, unless something changes?

After I collected a record class Kafue Flats lechwe the first morning up near Lochinvar, we flew later the same day to our camp at Chanjusi in the Valley for the start of serious hunting. On this my fifth safari, I had quite limited objectives (chiefly a hairy lion which I did not get), but even so, I was disappointed with the indifferent results this camp produced. The net outcome of a week's shooting in the legendary

Luangwa Valley was a mediocre greater kudu, a fair puku and a small impala shot for camp meat. Although lions came to bait, there was nothing worth taking. Elephant (which we were not hunting) are almost nonexistent, and the rhino are gone. The once famous valley is finished, or at best its days for trophy hunting are numbered. Its only hope would be to shut down hunting there for some period of time, but that is not politically or economically likely.

The third week of the safari was spent further west at Mulobezi. Here the situation was even worse. One record hartebeest in a week's hunting — and that was all. I could have had a fairly decent sable, but he would have been no improvement over the one I had, and I passed up a couple of very so-so roan in the 24-25 inch class. But even such animals as these were very scarce. However, in Mulobezi, I feel the almost total lack of game was due more to very dry weather that the area had been experiencing for some time than to poaching. The bulk of the game seemed to have shifted over into the Kafue National Park, where there was more water.

Sandwiched between the time spent in these two hunting areas were a few days further north near Lake Bangweulu. We did not see the lake itself, and I regret this, because with my love of history I would like to have visited some of the areas associated with David Livingstone and his work during the last century. But we did get into the great swamp that abuts it to the east, and in this and on the plains still further east, there was a fair amount of game. The number of species in the area is limited — sitatunga, black lechwe, roan, reedbuck, oribi — but they are found in good quantity. In addition, I am told there is the occasional lion.

Dave, who was also the safari company manager, had to return to Lusaka for a few days, so when our chartered flight landed, we were met at the airstrip near the main camp by a second professional, Peter Chipman. Half an hour later I shot a record class black lechwe; obviously, as with its larger cousin on the Kafue Flats, it is not much of a challenge. You can easily drive and drop one within an hour, so even though it does require an ability to shoot straight at somewhere between 150 and 250 yards, it certainly cannot be called hunting in the true sense of the word. Despite the fact that all the various lechwe

The Lake Bangweuleu area was fun to hunt and, in 1990, I took three nice trophies: A black lechwe, a reedbuck, and a Kafue Flats lechwe. My grandson, Charles, gladly posed with all the trophies.

make handsome trophies, I do not plan to hunt either the red or black again. And while I have never hunted them, I suspect that much the same is true of the Nile lechwe further north; they require good shooting, but not challenging hunting.

After this not very exciting "duty" had been completed we set out on a four-hour drive to a fly camp on the edge of the true swamp. It was there that I hoped to get a good sitatunga, one considerably larger than what I had shot previously.

I had successfully hunted this elusive and shy member of the bushbuck family on the Chobe River. Then we used a boat with a high superstructure from which I could see and shoot over the papyrus reeds — as long as we did not capsize and get dumped in among the Chobe's many crocodiles. At Bangweulu the method of hunting is different and probably a bit safer. Here one wades out through the swamp, walking gingerly on top of the floating bog to one of several small islands on which machans have been built in trees. Visibility is excellent and the chances of spotting a large bull are not bad. It sounds nice — and it does produce results — but no one can claim it is comfortable or easy hunting.

First of all the Lake Bangweulu area is very cold at night — I mean *very* cold — so wading through the icy water is not conducive to comfort. Some people use fishing waders, but they really are more trouble than they are worth. So the most common practice is simply to bite the bullet and wade out through the bone-chilling, knee-deep water barefoot and in shorts. Believe me when I say that this can be a character-building experience, especially when one must also face the somewhat remoter possibility of crocodiles even here, as well as bilharzia. The latter is a not-very-nice affliction caused by a parasitic liver fluke that is carried by snails found in the swamps of Africa. Upon my return to the States I went to have my blood checked to see whether I had made contact with this little beastie, but it was to no avail, because there are very few if any US based laboratories that can do the test. In any case I was assured that if I did contract bilharzia, it could be treated — for whatever comfort that knowledge was worth.

After the four-hour drive from main camp we arrived at what turned out to be a very comfortable fly camp. Actually, it did lack the effete plumbing we had grown used to in the others, but this minor inconvenience was compounded by the company's far more serious oversight in neglecting to replace the spent scotch whisky. However, after much grumbling on my part we managed to survive — just barely.

We wasted no time, and waded out that afternoon for a try from a machan. I made a mistake then that I would not repeat: Because the air was quite warm at that time of day, I was not thinking much about the cold water or the chill that would settle in as the sun started down in the late afternoon. Consequently, I only brought a light sweater to put on when it got cold. How I shivered and shook up in that machan. It was probably just as well that nothing shootable appeared, because I am not sure I could have held the rifle steady. In any event, except for a couple of females nothing came out, so we returned to camp at dusk, chilled to the bone with no scotch available to warm the inner man.

I was up at 3:45 the next morning and headed out with Peter to a different and more distant machan. If I thought the previous evening's wade had been cold, I really manifested a hunter's masochism during this predawn journey. However, this time I was carrying everything I had in the way of warm clothing: Long pants, sweater, windbreaker, socks and sneakers — all strung over my shoulders. Thus I came prepared and would put everything on when I reached the machan. So once having arrived and gotten myself ensconced, I was reasonably comfortable, but still dreading the wade back to camp which inevitably awaited us.

As the light began to increase, we made out several females, and eventually a fair male, perhaps 23-24 inches. I was tempted, but once again, this male was no better than what I already had, so we let him wander off undisturbed and unaware of the peril through which he had passed. So we eventually peeled off our shoes, socks and long trousers and labored back to the mainland, camp, and a welcome breakfast. That evening was a repetition of the previous night's experience with nothing shootable.

The next morning we were up again at 3:45 a.m. and managed to be in the machan about an hour later. It was still long before daylight and terribly cold as we huddled in the tree about 20 feet off the ground.

The stars were bright, and because it was only two nights after the full moon, we had fair visibility. Of course, in that light every bush seemed to be a sitatunga, and my excitement grew as the doves and the various swamp birds presently started to call. Africa was rousing itself from night.

Peter soon pointed out what looked like some barely visible clumps of shrubbery and said they were sitatunga. However, it was still too dark to make out whether there was anything big enough to interest us. It was not long before we could see that most of them were simply females feeding. Sitatunga are very territorial beasts, and the same male we had seen the morning before appeared and then wandered off, again leaving me with some misgivings.

Up to this point the safari had been so unproductive that I was growing increasingly pessimistic over my chances of finding a decent trophy here. I began to resign myself to another trip to the machan that evening and still another the next morning before we would have to leave and go back to main camp. Nothing worthwhile seemed to be out there as we gazed over the swamp that had now become quite visible in the morning light. Throughout the whole vigil we had been facing forward, looking north. That was the way we had positioned ourselves in the rather cramped machan. It held Peter and me, plus two trackers and a game ranger. Then one of the men, looking back in the direction from which we had waded out, nudged Peter, who in turn caught my attention. Over my right shoulder, probably about 75-100 yards away, there were two sitatunga feeding. One of them was a very good male. Without any hesitation Peter told me to shoot.

To avoid making a sound I had to aim from a very awkward position with my legs and hips still facing forward and my upper body twisted around, trying to sight on the big male. It was very bad, and when I fired, I knew right away that I had missed. But then as the two animals took off in opposite directions, all caution was thrown to the winds. I quickly hitched myself around while pumping another cartridge into the chamber of the 30.06. At this point an incredibly embarrassing, and even potentially dangerous, thing happened: My rifle went off! I was stunned by this accidental discharge as I worked the bolt, and I can only think that my finger must have inadvertently

Getting this Zambesi sitatunga at Lake Bangweuleu was difficult. I almost "froze."

pressed the trigger while I was trying to work myself into position for a second shot and pumping a fresh cartridge into the chamber at the same time. Fortunately, long years of training at the hands of my father paid off. The muzzle was pointed harmlessly away from everyone, and the bullet traveled up and out over the swamp.

The female had vanished, and the last I saw of the male was his disappearing behind a small island covered with thick brush and trees. I assumed that was the end of it and was very frustrated. However, in a moment he reappeared, having passed behind the island on the far side. To my astonishment he even stopped running and simply walked out into the open while angling away from us. Again I raised my rifle and fired, at what was now a considerably greater distance. I was pretty sure I saw him stumble, and Peter also thought I had hit him, but how badly we did not know. In any case, someone had to investigate — but not I.

I stayed in the machan with one of the men, while Peter climbed down from the tree and started across the treacherous bog with the other two. There is some danger in this, because quite often one is forced to walk on a floating bog, and there may be a considerable amount of water under it. Dave once told me of a professional who broke through and plunged to the very bottom (a nice experience with all the crocodiles around.) Fortunately for him, there was enough light to get back up through the hole he had made on the way down; otherwise, he would have drowned. I am sure Peter and the others were thinking of such things as they forged out into the swamp with the bog rising and falling under each step.

Before long I heard a yell; all three were still visible, so I knew no one had broken through or been grabbed by a crocodile. This meant the shout was one of triumph and could mean only one thing: They had found the sitatunga. And indeed they had. He was stone dead a few feet from where he had been when I fired my last shot.

Of course, I was exultant, but as in the case of my Botswana sitatunga in the bogs of the Chobe River, the responsibility for dragging this deceptively large animal back did not fall on me. Peter and the men managed to get him out to our main route where help soon arrived from the camp. The animal was then trussed up on a pole and carried by two men who struggled manfully toward *terra firma*. Why they did not plunge through some of the floating bog I will never know. In any case they eventually got him back safely, and after the necessary photographs we measured him at a bit over 25 inches. This was short of the Rowland Ward's record book, but I was very pleased nonetheless, because he was an old bull with a lot of bulk to his ivory-tipped horns. I was also greatly relieved not to have wade back into that swamp again.

Chapter 13

The Most Dangerous Game

After "Why do you hunt?" probably the most frequently asked question I hear is, "What is the most dangerous game in Africa?" Even though I have been on a fair number of safaris, I can not answer this with any real authority. I was momentarily threatened once by a rhino and chased in the car by an elephant we had been bothering. On another occasion I had the daylights scared out of me by a lion, and twice I have been charged by buffalo — once in an *unprovoked* charge. With all the time I have spent in Africa, my exposure to immediate danger in the field has been minimal. However, even among the professionals and others who have spent years in the bush and who have been in many tight situations, there is disagreement over what is actually the most dangerous game.

Apart from insects and snakes, the crocodile has almost certainly killed more people in Africa than any other animal, whereas many people would call the most dangerous mammal to be the hippo — never get between it and its water. But these are not really game animals. What most people are asking about is the relative danger of the Big Five: Elephant, rhino, buffalo, lion and leopard. Even among professionals and experts there is certainly no consensus on the subject.

I doubt whether few if any experienced African hands would select the rhino, although one killed such a veteran professional as Charles Cottar and another terribly injured Terry Matthews, a respected and experienced hunter of more recent years. Each of the other four certainly has their protagonists. J. A. Hunter, who was one of the legendary professionals in the middle decades of the 20th century, built a strong case for the leopard. Russell B. Aitken, the great American trophy hunter — one of the few foreigners, incidentally, who was allowed to make up his own safaris during the latter British days in Kenya — cast his vote for the elephant. The late Elgin T. Gates, another well known American sportsman, believed it to be the buffalo. Not to be outdone, Frederick Courteney Selous, perhaps the greatest hunter of all time, felt there was no contest; it is the lion. So there you are. Ask four qualified people, and you get four different answers. So I might as well throw in my own two cents. In a sentence, my vote would be for all *five* — under differing circumstances and from different perspectives.

If I were to base my judgment on which animal is most apt to cause trouble, I would have to vote for the rhino. The rhino — poor old fellow — is not highly endowed with gray matter. In fact, it is really left over from the early Stone Age. While it does have excellent hearing and a good sense of smell, it is practically blind. However, what it lacks in eyesight is in part compensated for by the ubiquitous tick birds that ride on its back. They can see — and see very well — so at the first approach of anything that might be dangerous these birds fly into the air and make an awful scene. Then old *faru* notices this, gets to its feet, and will charge anything it can vaguely make out: People, other animals, even safari cars. It can be very formidable. One night quite a few years ago I was watching the Lodge's water hole at Voi in Tsavo East, and there was a good collection of game under the flood lights — elephant, buffalo, and rhino. While these species seldom fight one another, they do like to establish a pecking order. Elephant can always intimidate the buffalo, and will sometimes attack and even kill a rhino when one of their calves seems to be threatened. But at that water hole I actually saw one of the great pachyderms back away when a rhino lowered his snout and started to advance.

The rhino is strong, short-tempered, and pretty stupid — a bad combination. Consequently, it probably becomes nasty more often than any of the other Big Five. In this sense it might be called the most dangerous. But the other side of the coin is that it often does not carry a charge through to its conclusion. Because its eyesight is so poor, evasive action is often possible — *unless* you are in thick brush. However, no one should ever take the rhino lightly; it is a cantankerous old brute that will not hesitate to demonstrate its ego. With reasonable

"Don't mess with me."

Leopard on the bait. It was smart enough to depart at the click of the camera.

care the hunter should be able to survive an encounter with one.

The elephant on the other hand is a different proposition. Apart from man and perhaps the great apes it is almost certainly the most intelligent animal in Africa; it is without question the largest, and its senses of hearing and scent are unequalled. If it has a chink in the armor, it is its eyesight, which, while not as bad as the rhino's, is not good. I have never been forced into a really tight corner by an elephant, but many people have, and many people have died, having been gored, tossed, crushed or generally annihilated, while others who lived to tell the tale have often been maimed for life. Russ Aitken believes that because the elephant is unquestionably the largest and the smartest of Africa's dangerous game, it presents the greatest threat to the hunter when angry. Cows are especially protective of their young, and nothing can be more intimidating than an enraged bull coming for you through bamboo that may be so thick that you cannot see him until he is almost on top of you, and it is often too late by then.

Elephants are unpredictable, and even though they generally leave you alone if you do not bother them, beware of the cow with her calf and beware of the wounded bull — watch out both for the bull and for his *askaris*. From the point of view of pure malicious size when stirred into hostile action, the elephant with all its intelligence and courage may indeed be the most dangerous game; at least many people who have hunted it think so. But it too can often be turned and forced to break off a charge, and, of course, it does present the largest target.

The leopard got the vote of J. A. Hunter. Very few experiences in Africa increase the heartbeat and flow of adrenaline the way going into thick brush after a wounded leopard does, but except for the very rare man-eater, an unwounded and unmolested leopard is virtually no threat to human beings. Unlike the rhino, elephant, and even buffalo, you are not going to get into trouble simply by stumbling on it while out shooting francolin. In fact, you will almost never even *see* one at close quarters under those conditions. Perhaps a female with cubs might be a threat — as Carl Akeley discovered — but still the danger from an unprovoked leopard attack is negligible. However, gut shoot one on a bait and then go after it — as you must — and you are walking into one of the most dangerous confrontations on earth. It will lead

The most dangerous game? A black rhinoceros (Kenya, 1983).

you into the very thickest cover and then wait. Unlike the lion, it will not growl as you get close, and you will not know it is there until you see a blurred streak of yellow and black hurtling toward you from 10 or 15 yards away. When this happens, someone usually gets hurt; it simply comes at too blinding a speed for most people to react. Nothing

— not even a cheetah — can get into high gear as *quickly* as the leopard. Probably the best defense in such cases is the shotgun; you just may be able to send a load of buckshot into its face in time to stop or turn it. When the leopard comes for you in thick brush, someone usually gets mauled, even though usually surviving. So if we are to judge the Big Five from the point of view of the one most apt to get *at* you when wounded, one's vote must go to the leopard — the supreme cat.

Then we come to its big cousin, the lion — *simba*. Much of what I have just said about the leopard also applies to the lion, but there are other considerations as well. When a wounded lion charges across the open from some distance away, which a leopard almost never does, if you keep your head *and shoot low*, he is not too hard to stop, but if he goes into thick brush, he is formidable indeed, being almost as fast as the leopard, and much bigger. To be sure he often warns you with a growl, giving you a second or two to get ready, but when this tawny rocket launches himself, he moves like lightning. And because he is much larger than the leopard, he can do a lot more damage when he lands on you. One bite can do you in very nicely.

Selous once said that it was not difficult to find men who had successfully hunted and killed thousands of elephant, thousands of rhino, and thousands of buffalo, but you would *never* find anyone who had killed even 100 lions. This is not literally true; several, including J. A. Hunter, have done so, but such people are few and far between, and this has not been due to any scarcity of lions, because until fairly recently they were very plentiful and were even considered vermin. The reason is that if you hunt them long enough, eventually, one is going to get you; it's as simple as that.

If we were to judge the relative danger of the Big Five, the bottom line would have to be: Which one has killed the most people. If this is the deciding criterion, the lion wins hands down. Walk through the Nairobi cemetery some Sunday afternoon, and you will see that "Killed By A Lion" is a frighteningly frequent epitaph.

However, there are reasons to question whether any one of these four is indeed the *most* dangerous of African game. The rhino, while most apt to give you trouble, is usually the easiest to escape. The elephant, on the other hand, because it does not possess an inherently

Whether or not you vote for elephant as "the most dangerous" game, it certainly is the largest.

Another black rhino, letting us know that we were getting too close.

hostile nature, will probably leave you alone if you do the same with it. Also, if you are after a big bull, you are more apt to deliver a lethal first shot, because he presents the largest target, and in the event of a charge even if you miss the brain, a head shot hitting anywhere near it will usually turn him. Cats are soft-skinned and can at least be disabled more easily than the rhino or elephant. In fact, in a charge any one of these four animals can frequently be turned, even if you do not immediately stop one. Hit it hard and it will often break off. The rhino is usually not in earnest when it starts a charge, but even when it is, it too can frequently be turned by a shot that may not be immediately fatal; the same can be said of lion and leopard, but do not count on it. In the case of the leopard, because of its relatively small size and the help of modern antibiotics, even if mauled, the victim usually survives. So these four are all dangerous, very dangerous, but each has its weakness. Then there is *mbogo*, the Cape buffalo, the African animal I fear more than any other.

The bull is one of the largest wild bovines in the world — as far as I know, he is exceeded in size only by the Asiatic gaur. He weighs close to a ton and is all muscle. Generally, in fact almost always, he is a gentleman, and an unprovoked attack, while not unknown, is rare. When it does happen, it is almost always the result of stumbling on a cow and calf or on some old bull, rousting it from sleep in the bush or from its favorite mud hole. As will be recounted later, Dave and I were once charged without provocation by a lone bull. The buffalo has certainly killed fewer people than either elephant or lion, and probably has not even tried to kill as many as leopard or rhino. So if one is to judge the ultimate danger of the Big Five on the basis of the hunter's risk of being attacked, it seems to me that the buffalo must rank at the bottom of the list.

It is not all that hard to kill *if* you place your first shot correctly, and when you do wound one, nine times out of 10 it will run as most other animals will. But go after a wounded bull, perhaps hitting him several more times with those 510-grain bullets; get his blood hot, and when he is hurting enough and knows he cannot escape, he will come to bay. When that happens there will be big trouble. Sometimes, he doubles back on his track and comes at you from behind, a

Taking a hippo is easy. It is hard to believe that they can be so dangerous. But they are.

disconcerting experience to say the least. At other times, the bull will simply wait until he believes he has you in a bad spot and then charge. When *mbogo* raises his snout and starts grunting, he comes like an express train and is just about as hard to stop. Your best chance lies in firing before he can really get started.

While the other four can often be turned in a charge, this is not true of the buffalo. It does not charge often, but when it does, it means to kill you. There are only two ways you can avoid that unhappy outcome: Either kill the buff first or get up a tree fast. You will not discourage it or make it break off and turn away. When a male comes, it is very difficult to stop with a head shot, because of the huge boss of horn protecting much of his skull. Although I did see Dave Ommanney do it — but then Dave is a professional. You can shoot a bull's heart out or rip up his lungs, but even that generally does not do the job in time. In 1913 my father put a .470 bullet through the heart of a buffalo

— fortunately not a charging one — and it *still* ran about 100 yards before going down. Yes, it is bad news when the buffalo decides that it is time to stop running and turns to hunt the hunter.

The buffalo also has an incredible ability to hold lead. Hit it right the first time, and it will die as easily as an impala, but be sure you do. If it is only wounded, subsequent shots, even many of them, have remarkably little effect. In 1971 my son, Henry, took on a bull. His first shot was a bit too far back. The buff then ran, and the fat was in the fire. Henry and Dave followed while Randy and I waited in the hunting car. Over the next 20 minutes we heard Henry's .458 and Dave's .470 go off 18 — yes, 18 — times. Finally, the buffalo went down, and upon subsequent examination, 14 shots were found to have hit him — and those were 510-grain bullets! Any number of them should have been fatal, but the buff simply did not know that he was dead. Dave said that if he had not fallen on that last shot, he was ready to come for them. Yes, this animal is one tough character.

Pay your money, and take your choice. Is the most dangerous game the rhino that is the one most apt to charge? Is it the elephant, the largest and most intelligent of the five, and a fearsome antagonist when crashing toward you through the heavy brush? Is it the leopard, when it is almost impossible even to get your rifle on it as it breaks from cover a few yards away and streaks toward you almost at the speed of light? Is it the lion, that like its smaller cousin waits under cover and then comes at blinding speed with a coughing grunt, adding several hundred pounds to that of the leopard? Or is it a buffalo, that peace-loving fellow who likes nothing better than to wallow in the mud, but who, when he finally reaches his limit and charges, is so tough as to be almost impossible to stop before he reaches you?

Take your choice and then hope you never have to prove you were right.

Chapter 14

Eden Regained

Initially, I set out to write an *apologia* for hunting, to try to describe the really indescribable excitement of an old time safari and then to recount my own hunting experiences. However, there is a very real part of the African scene to which I have only alluded: Game parks and preserves. In any consideration of African wildlife something should be said about these, because this is where most game is actually seen and photographed today, and also because they represent one realistic hope for the ultimate survival of Africa's wild animals.

Game parks, mostly in Kenya and Tanzania, range in size from the very small Nairobi National Park, which is only about 10 miles out of the city, to the almost 8,000 square miles of the combined eastern and western sections of Tsavo National Park, halfway between Nairobi and the coast. There are others, notably the remarkable Kruger National Park in the Republic of South Africa, but it is in Kenya and Tanzania that the park system has been developed to the greatest degree.

These parks are not like the San Diego zoo (wonderful as that is in the heart of urban America), nor are the animals fed or cared for by man — an exception being the Animal Orphanage attached to the Nairobi National Park. Kruger is fenced, as are three sides of Nairobi, but except for these (as far as I know) the parks are all open. This allows the animals complete freedom to come and go as they please, most of them learning very quickly to be "pleased" to stay within the park confines, that protect them from trophy hunters, even if not from poachers.

In the passage of time with the almost inevitable depletion of Africa's wild habitat, its parks may provide the only refuge left for the game. They will provide a refuge *if* — and this is a big "if" — the

Cheetah on the Serengeti.

Lions in trees. Lake Manyara, 1987.

A superb bushbuck, but he's at Treetops. This may not be far off the world record.

Approaching thunderstorm at Maswa, Tanzania.

authorities are able and *willing* to resist the ever-increasing pressure for more human living space and more grazing land for domestic animals. Amboseli has already been reduced to a mere shadow of what it once was, while even the little that is left is open to Masai cattle.

The time will come when large parks like Tsavo will need artificial water holes. From before recorded history this necessity of life has been the name of the game for African animals; they have always followed the water in their migrations. Incidentally, one of the last of the truly great migrations can be still be seen in the latter part of July and beginning of August in the Masai Mara just north of the Serengeti. Perhaps 1,000,000 wildebeest, accompanied by thousands of zebra, come north each year and then begin to move south again with the little rains of October and November. They are, of course, accompanied by the predators, so it is a fantastic sight.

As people crowd in and around the parks, true migration will be impossible, especially for elephants, so water holes will have to be created, as they already are on the South African game ranches on the Great Karroo. However, digging the wells and providing and maintaining proper piping will cost money; let us hope it is there.

If you want game photography, go to the parks, where, incidentally, most of the living game pictures in this book were taken. While the animals are not tame, they have grown used to motorized vehicles, and it is possible to drive right up to a pride of lions or a herd of eland and photograph to your heart's content. If you have the time and are patient, you can witness the whole life cycle — mating, birth, feeding, predation and death. The larger parks have comfortable lodges in which to stay, and several of these such as the smaller, yet superb, Ark and Treetops, afford opportunity for game viewing right from the buildings.

It is possible to be a bit more primitive in your use of the parks. Some have private tented camps within or just outside park boundaries. To some extent these try to approximate the old safari life; at least they have evening campfires and provide only canvas between you in your tent and the various wild animals outside. Phyllis and I had an interesting experience in 1983. We were at Cottar's Camp just outside the Mara with Arthur and Roberta Walmsley, two friends

This hyena knows how to relax in the Ngorongoro crater.

Grevy's zebra at Samburu. They are beautiful, but not bright when compared with their cousins, the Burchell's zebras found farther south.

from Connecticut who also were our bishop and his wife. In the middle of the night, Phyllis suddenly leaped into my bed, whispering that she had felt something *big* brushing up against her through the canvas. I was skeptical to say the least, but to reassure her, not too graciously I got up and flashed a light outside. I did not tell her that I heard a leopard calling some distance away, but I saw no sign of anything "big" near by. She was finally coaxed back to her own bed, but at breakfast the next morning Roberta Walmsley announced that exactly the same thing had happened in their tent which was next in line to ours. Upon examination we did indeed find buffalo tracks right outside the two tent walls. Perhaps it is just as well that my curiosity had not been sufficient for me to investigate more extensively in the dark.

Except for my last two safaris, we started all our trips in Kenya and over the years have visited every park except Marsabit and Meru. In addition we have gone into Ngorongoro Crater, the Serengeti, and Manyara in Tanzania. Each has its own character, and they all contribute to the survival of the game.

Samburu, a game preserve not visited as often as the Mara or Tsavo, is one of the most remarkable. It is in a semidesert area up toward Kenya's Northern Frontier District. When we went there in 1990, we stayed at Larsen's Camp, a private tented camp in the preserve. Samburu is not noted for large herds, especially during excessive dry spells. But when we were there, game was abundant: Elephant, gerenuk, impala, oryx, grant's gazelle, Grevy zebra, and the reticulated giraffe (the last two species found only in northern Kenya), and finally many tiny dik-diks. For some reason there did not seem to be many if any predators — at least we saw no sign of any. This may be why the game is so tame and more at peace than any I have seen elsewhere in Africa. It was remarkable the way one could drive right up to elephants — even cows with calves — with no sign of alarm on their parts. It was almost as though one was wandering through the Garden of Eden before the Fall. At the time I said that I would have to write a chapter on this and call it *Eden Regained*.

If Samburu can be called the Garden of Eden, Ngorongoro must be likened to Noah's Ark. With a few notable exceptions (giraffe, oryx, gerenuk, greater and lesser kudu, roan and topi), every species of big

Preparing a new generation. David Ommanney introduces the author's nine-year-old grandson to the .22.

game indigenous to northern Tanzania is found there. Ngorongoro is a huge crater about 2000 feet deep and 15 miles across. Actually, it is not a crater at all, but a caldera, which I am told is what is left of the cavity created by a long-dead volcano. In any case it is a great hole on the top of a mountain. In Ngorongoro can be found as incredible a collection of game for such a small area as anywhere in Africa, at least anywhere I have been. Perhaps one reason for this is the topography; it is quite a climb up to the ridge and then down into the "crater" itself, so the game tends to stay put. Amazingly, the number of animals and the supply of food and water appear to stay remarkably in balance, the wildlife never seeming to exceed the environment's ability to feed it. Also, due to its isolated location, it must intimidate poachers, because it has to be almost impossible for them to carry out their nefarious work undetected.

Although Ngorongoro is very small, I suspect that because of its geography it may well end up being the last refuge for big game after everything else is gone. Animals, both predators and their prey, can and do live out their whole life span within the crater.

There is, however, one very real threat to its lions. Because of Ngorongoro's isolation and small size there are alarming indications that inbreeding has been developing over the past years to the extent that the population is being seriously endangered. This is such a real problem that at the time of this writing there is talk of introducing new blood by bringing some lions into the preserve from the outside.

In any case big game hunting might soon be a glorious page in Africa's history. Before long the advance of civilization will take all the open grazing land away from the wildlife. Perhaps Samburu and Ngorongoro, along with Africa's other parks and preserves, will survive and with them a small vestige of what once was. Let us hope so.

Chapter 15

An Afternoon In the Sun

"*Chui!*" We heard a quiet but urgent tap on the top of the car and when we stopped, the tracker whispered this one word to John Northcote. This started a train of events that culminated in one of the high points of my African hunting.

The leopard is the ultimate — the supreme — cat. Except when mating, the male is almost always alone or, in the case of a female, with her cubs. Unlike the lion it is a solo hunter, almost exclusively nocturnal in its habits, so it is seldom seen by the casual observer or tourist. When one is occasionally spotted in a game park, it causes great excitement; the word spreads and cars converge from every direction. Park leopards are so used to this sort of thing that they usually sleep through it, but in big game hunting areas it is quite another story.

Because they are so rarely seen, it was believed that leopards were becoming scarce. They were even added to the Endangered Species list for several years, before being transferred to *Cites II*, the Threatened list. Actually, today there are almost certainly more leopards in Africa than lions. However, the latter are easily seen in the parks — usually stretched out under some acacia tree in the hot sun and sleeping off a big feed. So most people think they still survive in great numbers. They do not, and a good male is becoming harder and harder to get on a hunting safari — well do I know. I am certain that leopards will be around in the wild long after lions are found only in the preserves, circuses, and zoos. For some time leopards were mercilessly poached for their spotted skins, but now that market has been pretty well shut down through the Endangered Species Act, they are making an excellent comeback. It has finally penetrated the minds of the powers that be that the leopard population can easily stand — even benefit from — the relatively small culling resulting from sport

Raising a leopard bait (1971).

hunting. Consequently, just recently it has again become possible to shoot leopard in those countries where it is clearly not endangered and then bring the skin back legally to the United States. This requires some advance red tape with our Department of the Interior, but it is really not very difficult to get the clearance. And it is certainly worth the effort.

After preparing the bait and a five hour wait in the sun, this good leopard was my reward (Botswana, 1987).

In all the time I had spent in Africa I had never even *seen* a living leopard in the wild, never mind getting my sights on one. On our first safari (Tanzania) my son Randy shot a nice tom from a blind. Later in the same trip my other son photographed one coming to bait. But *I* had not seen one. It is true that I had not seriously hunted them. On my first trip I wanted a lion, so Randy got the crack at the leopard. In 1975 and 1983 they were on the Endangered Species List. In 1987, even though they had been removed from that, my chances of getting one in Botswana were slim. At the time it was illegal to bait for cats, and tracking a leopard is next to impossible. In Botswana, unless you drive a vehicle through the Kalahari, which I believe is closed to hunting as of this writing, about the only chance you have is to bump into one by happenstance when looking for other game. This is exactly how I finally made eye contact with *chui*.

In most places where leopards are successfully hunted, the normal

Kyosi getting ready to hang a leopard bait. This was in 1975 in a different country. Throughout Africa, the procedure can be somewhat the same.

procedure is to bait them — their favorite is the warthog. If a leopard is working in the area, you must be willing to get up long before daylight and sit motionless in a blind for the first hour or so after the sun comes up and then return for the last hour before it goes down. You must be

The leopard blind as it appeared from the bait. Would the leopard spot it?

willing to do this day in and day out in order to have at least an even chance of getting one. But none of this was allowed in Botswana, so we had pretty much put leopards out of mind.

That morning we had started off at a very civilized hour after a good English breakfast. The sun had long been up, and I was in the lead car with John Northcote and his trackers. My wife and our friend followed in the second car with Dave Ommanney. I do not remember what we were looking for — very possibly greater kudu or lion, both of which I was still trying to improve over what I had already taken. In any case, about the last thing we expected to run into was a leopard. Then we heard the tap on the car roof and the whispered word, *"chui"* — leopard.

I say "we" heard it; John did; I did not. However, over the months spent on several safaris I had finally learned to grab my rifle and pile out of the car quickly, asking questions later. But this time, after looking around helplessly for a moment or two and seeing nothing, I asked

John what it was. His reply was simply, "Leopard!" "Where?" I asked with a note of urgency in my voice. He did not have to answer, for at that moment I saw the great cat leap down from high in a tree and immediately disappear into the underbrush. Finally, I had actually seen a leopard in the wild, but he was gone. Too bad.

When we wandered over to see what it had been all about, we assumed that it had been sleeping the day away high up on a limb. However, to our surprise we saw a partially eaten warthog, jammed into a crotch about 15 feet off the ground. This was a heaven-sent opportunity, because, while it was illegal to set up a bait in Botswana, there was no law against sitting *over a kill*. We had not disturbed it in any way, so John and Dave were pretty sure it would return. They then set about building a blind about 40 yards from the tree.

When John and I had hidden ourselves in this, Dave left with the girls. The trackers drove our car off, and we settled down for what would either be a very short or a very long wait. Because this big male had not been particularly disturbed and might still be hungry, there was a good chance that he would return as soon as he saw the cars leave. Or, if he had had a fairly good meal, he might have just run off and gone to sleep. In which case he could be expected back about sundown. We simply had to wait and see.

When sitting over a kill or a bait for leopard you must remain absolutely silent and motionless, because it has incredible eyesight and hearing. When my son photographed that one in 1971, he got just one picture, because it heard the click of the camera and was gone. Consequently, I sat with the safety off — afraid that if I waited until it came, even a possible click in throwing it off might scare the leopard away before I had a chance to shoot. I was using a .300 magnum with a soft point in the chamber, just perfect for what I needed.

The leopard did not come back right away, so we resigned ourselves to a long wait in the African sun. Of course, when you must not move, you get restless, cramps develop, and your body seems to scream out to get up and stretch, but you have to endure it if you are to have any chance with a leopard. For me the time dragged endlessly — one hour, two hours, three hours, four hours, and so on into the afternoon. Meanwhile John was stretched out on the ground behind and seemed to be asleep. I doubt if he really was, but he certainly was much more comfortable than I. I had to watch the warthog almost continuously. If the leopard returned, he would come soundlessly. Frankly, I did not hold out much hope, although I learned later that both John and Dave had been pretty sure that he would indeed return, but would this be before or after the sun went down?

Despite myself, my head nodded, and from time to time I almost dropped off. I would jerk back to life, cast a glance toward the tree, see nothing but the warthog, and then resume my aching state of semiconsciousness. About 5 p.m., over six hours after we had started our vigil, John stirred and touched my arm. I looked first at him, then at the warthog, but still no leopard. Why had he done this? What was he trying to tell me? It would have done no good to whisper, because I have lost much of my hearing and am quite handicapped in communicating quietly in the presence of game. I was partly conscious of having heard *something* just before he poked me. I could not remember what it was — certainly it was not the leopard. He would come in absolute silence. Still there had been something out of place that had not quite registered in my somnolent state. Needless to say, I immediately become more alert. Within a minute, *the leopard was back in the tree.*

He had come without a sound, no sound at all. Suddenly he was just there. I shifted the rifle slowly and quietly to my shoulder and sighted through the scope. However, there was a large limb shielding its shoulder, and I could not shoot; so I had to wait. The leopard, a big male, was looking around cautiously making sure everything was all right before he started to feed. I was not nervous, because somehow I knew I had him. Sooner or later he would expose his shoulder. When this happened, I fired. At the crack of the rifle I saw him drop out of the tree with all four feet straight up in the air. Then there was a loud thud, followed by silence.

I turned to John, who had been watching me aim and shoot, but had not been able to see the leopard from where he was sitting. He simply smiled and said, "Well, it sounded good." However, he also said we should wait a few minutes before going for a look. He explained then that what he had heard when he poked me and what had not

Randy with his leopard (Kisigo, 1971).

quite registered in my consciousness had been the alarm call of a francolin. When he heard this, he knew the leopard was coming and tried to alert me. I had heard the bird's cackle too, but had hardly noticed it, not having any idea what it meant.

Finally we rose, I with my .300 magnum (safety off), and John with his 12-gauge shotgun loaded with buckshot. The latter was reassuring at the time, but little did I know that a few days later when we went out to the river with Dave for some dove shooting, John's shotgun would break down. Anyway, we worked forward very cautiously, but had only gone a few yards when he calmly said, "There he is." Indeed, there he was, stretched out below the tree right where he had fallen. However, we did not relax — too many people have been killed in Africa by "dead" animals. Sure enough after we had watched him for a moment, there was a slight movement of his mouth, perhaps an attempt to growl. John wanted it to be a one-shot kill, but I was taking no chances and put a finishing bullet high into his back.

It was probably unnecessary, but I was taking no chances either of losing him or getting chewed up. My own hide was worth more than sparing the leopard's hide another bullet hole.

The trackers, who had heard the shots, soon brought the car around. We took pictures in the late afternoon sun, loaded this gorgeous trophy into it, and headed back to camp. Needless to say, I was in a state of complete euphoria.

I really had no right getting a leopard under those circumstances, especially a large tom that would ultimately make the record book. You do not often see them the way we did and then have them conveniently leave a kill in the tree when we were not allowed to set baits ourselves. Everything fell together; it was another case of my old Canadian guide's philosophy: "I guess his time was up."

Strangely enough, the next time I saw a leopard in the wild was in the Transvaal 10 years later. As the afternoon was drawing to a close and as we were moving slowly along a dirt road, I had a glimpse of a large animal crossing the road a couple of hundred yards in front of us. It was only a glimpse, and it disappeared immediately. I said, "If I didn't know better I would say that I had seen a leopard." If this were true, it would have been a *most* unusual event on a South African game ranch. In any case when we arrived at the spot, there were the unmistakable fresh tracks of *chui*.

Chapter 16

The Soul of Africa

For most people who hunt in Africa, at least for those who are newcomers to big game hunting, their prime objective is almost always *simba*, the lion. For many a lion is the very soul of the African wild. There is no sound quite like the lion's roar, especially when you are lying in bed, listening to the night sounds coming off the veldt. And when he is finally gone — if that should ever happen — the soul of Africa will indeed be lost.

The lion is not the largest of the great cats. The Siberian tiger, from which no human being has, to my knowledge, ever survived a mauling, is much heavier. It can weigh up to 700 pounds. His somewhat smaller cousin, a big male Bengal tiger, often reaches 500, whereas a large African lion tips the scales at 450. There have been reports of exceptional ones going as high as 550 or more. I have even heard of one shot by a woman that weighed 598 pounds, but such magnificent trophies are rare indeed. However, although usually somewhat smaller than the tiger, the lion has rightly earned the title "King of the Beasts" — at least king of the predators. I make this qualification because in terms of size, intelligence, and virtual immunity from attack by other animals (except man) the African elephant is truly the king. However, most people associate royalty in the animal kingdom with the lion. Even when plentiful, the tiger was rarely seen for more than an instant. After all, it is largely nocturnal. And when it is seen in the daylight, more often than not, it is running, perhaps because as Jim Corbett said, "He is a wise fool." The lion *acts* like a king — typically sprawled under some flat-topped thorn tree, surrounded by his pride and with an air of utter arrogance. At times he can show incredible, perhaps foolhardy, courage — something which kings are meant to do in battle — and when a big lion has developed a great mane, he is certainly the very image of royalty.

Of course, there is a somewhat less than regal side to the lion as well. Its eating habits do not have the air of *noblesse oblige.* For one thing the larder is almost always provided by the ladies of the pride, who then dutifully step aside while His Majesty dines to complete satisfaction. Lions are not great hunters; the ratio of success to failure is far below that of the wild dog or even *fisi*, the despised hyena. As a result our king is not choosy about what he eats; even carrion killed by hyenas will do very nicely. And with it all, when times get rough, and when food is really scare, he is not above grabbing a cub or two from his own pride. Speaking of cubs, when an old pride leader is finally and inevitably dethroned in battle and either killed or driven out by a younger prime male, the newcomer systematically kills all existing cubs in the pride — not an appealing custom. However, the lion is still the king, and it is the rare African hunter — sportsman or professional — who feels he has really joined the ranks until he has brought one down.

I shot a mature male on my first safari, but he had a very meager mane. I often said that our pet Maine coon cat had a better mane than that lion. I tried to better him in 1975 without even seeing a male. There were no lions where we were in South Africa. In 1987, I saw two very nice ones, narrowly missing a chance for a shot on one and then slightly wounding a second. In 1990 I passed up two immature males and did the same in 1993 on a relatively maneless male. So I had a frustrating time with *simba*, yet just hunting him has been a exciting experience.

I barely shot my one lion in 1971. My sons and I started hunting in the Kisigo area of central Tanzania, where we bagged sable, leopard, and greater kudu. We baited, but saw no lion at all. When we moved north into Maswa, east of the Victoria Nyanza, it was a very different story. During a period of 10 days we counted 63 lions. To be sure, most were lionesses and cubs, and the few males were by and large immature or with very scruffy manes; but at least we were finding lions. We did see one with a fair mane — feeding on a buffalo we had hung — and it stayed around for several days, becoming a bone of contention between David Ommanney and myself. I thought he had more than a

Hungry and getting ready for the afternoon hunt.

Some times a lion's fancy turns to things other than hunting, eating, or sleeping.

Every book has one photo of "His royal majesty, the king of beasts."

fair mane; he certainly was good enough for me on my first safari. But because we still had a week or so left and because we were seeing lots of lion, Dave persuaded me not to shoot. I was not happy about this, but still had hopes that we would see one of those big black-maned beauties of every client's dreams.

Building a lion blind.

One by one the days slipped by, and we saw nothing as good as "George" (the name we had attached to that disputed lion). I was getting quite anxious and would not let Dave forget what we had let go by default. At the time I assumed that this would be my one and only trip to Africa, and the thought of returning home without a lion really rankled. Throughout my childhood I had sat enthralled, listening over and over again to my father's account of shooting four lions by moonlight in one night — all within 10 — 12 feet of the *boma* in which he and one very frightened gun bearer were waiting. Now it began to look as though I might well return empty-handed. The thought rankled.

Then one morning, two days before we were due to break camp and head back to Arusha, we found number 64 working on a bait. Dave looked at him with scorn. While he was a big bodied male, he did not have a good mane (although certainly much better than many of the almost maneless lions that were shot over the years in the

147

Northern Frontier District in Kenya). We argued for a while, and then turned away after I had been made to feel terribly guilty over even wanting to shoot this "hyena," as Dave called him. However, he had no idea how deeply the desire for a lion had permeated my soul.

We cruised about for the rest of the morning and eventually returned to camp for lunch. Throughout the trip back and then during lunch itself, I was sulking, with lots of fuming going on inside. I was really being quite childish and should simply have had the gumption to come right out and say that I wanted that lion — period. Of course, Dave could still have refused (the professional always has the final say), but I don't think he would have. He knew something was bothering me, and when I swallowed my pride after lunch and finally did say that I would like to go for him, he reluctantly agreed. I guess it had gradually sunk in just how much this meant to me in those early days of African hunting — right or wrong. I am sure he hoped the lion would be gone by the time we got back to the bait, but such was not the case.

It took us about half an hour to reach the spot, and sure enough, our lion was still there, lying under the suspended buffalo and keeping the vultures away. Dave rightly insisted that if I were going to shoot, I would have to do so in a reasonably sporting manner, so we decided on some subterfuge.

The first thing we did was to drive him from the bait, and he ran off quickly enough. Then we drove out of sight and set our plan into motion. My sons, along with the trackers, were in the car with us. We put the boys in the back with one tracker. Then the second took the wheel with Dave and me sitting beside him in the front.

Driving obliquely toward the bait — pretty sure the lion was watching us from cover — we got to within about 100 yards of the bait. Then Dave and I rolled out the far side of the vehicle and got down behind a large fallen tree, thus concealing us from the direction of the bait. The car continued on with the trackers and my sons. We figured we must have fooled the lion, because we doubted that he could count that well.

We were lying behind the fallen tree; I had my head down with the .375 resting on the ground beside me, and Dave was reading a

Simba. This is what the author came for in 1971.

book. We had not been there five minutes before he looked over the log and casually remarked, "He's back." I remained surprisingly calm as I raised the rifle very slowly and rested my hand on the log. It was perfect: shooting from a prone position with a steady hand rest, and a broadside shot at a lion standing in the open at about 100 yards. When I fired, he dropped in his tracks.

However, that was not quite the end of it. It later turned out that his back was broken, so he was not going anywhere, but we did not know that then. Needless to say we approached very carefully, keeping out of sight and to the rear. It was soon obvious that this lion was far from dead, so Dave told me to shoot again, aiming for a spot between the shoulder blades. When I fired, he immediately whirled and bit where the bullet had struck. A lion's vitality is so great that it took two or three more carefully placed shots before he finally quit. At this I quietly said, "*Kwa heri*" — good-bye.

I had my lion, but it was with mixed emotions. I was elated beyond measure, but at the same time feeling a bit ashamed, because I knew Dave would have respected me more had I simply passed this one up. There was also a touch of sadness as I gazed down on the fallen monarch. I always feel this way after shooting an animal, but especially this time. All things being considered, I have no regrets. Since then I have hunted lions relentlessly, coming close in Botswana and even passing up maneless males later, but I imagine another lion is not to be.

In the meantime, along with the epitaph on the grave of Ashurbanipal, the great king of ancient Assyria, I can truthfully say, "I have killed the lion."

Chapter 17

The Way It Was

The following excerpt is from an article written by my father, H. Lloyd Folsom, for the Cloyne School alumni magazine. Two years after his graduation from Yale he took a six month's safari to Kenya — then British East Africa — with two classmates: His former roommate, Jack Terry, and another close friend, Lyman Hine.

It was 1913, just before the world went mad. Karen von Blixen would be moving to Kenya that year; Elspeth Huxley was still a child running around with her Nandi playmates among the flame trees of Thika; Lord Delamere was fast becoming the premier settler in BEA; and the Muthaiga Club was the arena for the Empire at play.

The trip my father took was a foot safari, complete with scores of porters and under the rather loose direction of his white hunter, George Outram, who, incidentally, would be killed by a lion near Taveta in 1922. I say "loose direction," because things were not as closely regulated in those days. Today no client would be allowed to go out alone even for a Thomson's gazelle, never mind into a *boma* at night with only a gun bearer for company to await the possible arrival of lions on a zebra bait. But things were different then. That is the way it was; perhaps we can get a glimpse of the old days from my father's account. Incidentally, I have not changed either his punctuation or spelling.

"Our first camp on these plains [in the area of the North Ewaso Nyero River not far from Narok HTF] was situated in a point of open woods that jutted out into the plain… There was a small provision store at this point on the Guaso Neyro River and we soon went over to pay a call upon the lone storekeeper. He immediately made us sit up and take notice by informing us that there were plenty of lions about

A foot safari in 1913. Sixth from the front is the author's father, riding on a mule.

and that they had been doing considerable damage among the cattle, donkeys, and sheep of the natives thereabout. We were all enthusiasm at once and had a long *Shauri* (conference) as to the best way of getting them. We thought of getting our boys together and beating a likely place for them and we thought of visiting baits at daylight, but George Outram, our white hunter came forward and said to build a *boma* for them. A *boma* for this purpose consists of a pile of thorn branches in front of some bait. You get inside of this and wait for the lions to come — at night. The bait is usually a zebra because you can make out his stripes in the darkness. This may not be the most dangerous way of hunting the lions, but it certainly is the most interesting, as well as exciting, of all the methods we tried. [Probably *the* most dangerous was the long-outlawed coursing of lions — running them down by horseback, leaping off when they came to bay, and then shooting them as they charged! HTF] Lyman Hine went out and shot a zebra which was to be the bait. The storekeeper then loaned us oxen and the zebra was ignominiously hauled by his hind legs over the veldt in a great circle, finally winding up at the *boma*... This dragging of the bait is naturally a good thing, because a lion is almost sure to cross it somewhere, get the scent, follow it up and investigate...

"[After unsuccessful vigils on two successive nights] the equatorial sun had had a good deal of play upon the body of the dead zebra and the latter was beginning to assert himself very freely, and this is just what the lion likes...

"Now my gunbearer and I arrived at sundown the next evening. I had grave doubts as to whether I wanted to spend the night on the ground within seven feet of that zebra or not but I soon forgot entirely about it — for there were other things to take all my attention.

"It was now just dark enough to be unable to see one's sights over the barrel of the rifle and although there was a moon it was rather clouded and consequently there was very little light. Suddenly a lion grunted quite close by and then another and then another, and then — silence, except for the incessant singing of the frogs in the nearby swamp. I began to get pretty nervous and in the darkness I could just catch a sickly kind of smile from the gunbearer beside me. I was just beginning to wonder what on earth had made me come down from a safe home, all the way out there to do this sort of thing when the gunbearer clutched me. And hurriedly peering out through the bushes I saw a lioness in the act of settling down over the bait, then slowly raising the big double-barreled .470 I pointed for what I supposed was well down on her fore shoulder and fired. There was a blinding flash — a terrific report and everything on earth seemed to be loose at once. She gave a series of terrible coughing growls which made me chilly all over. When my eyes had recovered from the flash made by the gun I looked out once more at the bait. She was gone. Then came the singing of the frogs the same as before and all was silence otherwise. [Something my father did not include in this article for his school alumni magazine was the fact that when daylight finally came, the gun bearer had to relieve himself. He pushed the bush in the entranceway aside and proceeded to empty his bladder — right on top of the dead lioness. He gave quite a start and leapt back into the *boma*. HTF]

"Of course I supposed that the big report would end all other

Chania Falls in Kenya from the Blue Posts Hotel in 1913. Compare this picture with one taken 70 years later shown below.

Camp in 1913. Compare it to the one shown below, also 70 years later. In some places, little has changed.

Three of the four lions shot by the author's father from the *boma* and in the moonlight.

The *boma* and the zebra bait in 1913.

Simba M'Kubwa — the great lion.

My father, H. Lloyd Folsom with a small warthog.

lion shooting for most of that night, but not at all. [lions were vermin in those days, and one was allowed to shoot as many as desired, of either sex. HTF] In a very few moments both the gunbearers and I were aware of something — we did not know exactly what — that made us both listen for all that we were worth. My heart seemed to be making an awful noise and even breathing seemed unpardonable. Then quiet footsteps came directly behind us and I wheeled around and faced the back of the *boma*. Instantly there came a growl and the lion began circling us. This was scary work for of course we could only see through the opening in front. When the lion came opposite I could only make out a swiftly-moving shape and held my fire. The gunbearers had my second rifle, a Remington Automatic .35 calibre, and I told him to be all ready with it, for I was afraid the brute might spring upon the top of the *boma* and come through upon us, which would not be especially pleasant. We did not care so much if he were going to try the very improbable thing of coming though the thorn sides of the *boma* because that would take him several seconds and the double rifle and the Remington Automatic would not do his face any good at that distance. However, on the second or third time round he stopped at the bait and I could just make him out. The gunbearers whispered: '*Simba manamumi, bwana, upaysi*' — Male lion, master, hurry. Again I fired and the big bullet struck into his shoulder crushing it and going through the lungs out through the other side. The shock must have been terrific. It knocked him down but he was able to pick himself up and taking one spring he fell and lay still.

"A lioness acted in much the same way. She circled the *boma* and told us all sorts of nice things but would not stop at the bait. She did stop a little beyond, however, and just then there was a little more light, due to the moon coming through the clouds, making her visible. I fired. She gave a big growl and came at the *boma*. I fired again and hit her. However, these bullets did not kill her outright. She had to be finished in the morning that is the dangerous part of *boma* shooting, because although the lion may be very close when you fire, it is not always possible to put the bullet in the right place, on account of the darkness. Then the lion goes to the thickest brush he can find until you come upon him in the morning — then look out!

My father was only 25 years old when he went on that 1925 safari, but he earned the nickname *Bwana M'Kubwa*.

"Another big lion was killed the same night, but the most remarkable incident of all was yet to come — before daylight a lioness came. She came quickly without a sound, sprang upon the bait, turned it around so that the head and shoulders would face the *boma*. Then she got down behind it and started to eat. After doing this she really seemed to know and realize that she was safer with the bait facing us lengthwise than when it was broadside to us. Using soft nose bullets I was unable to shoot through the bait lengthwise and thus hit her on the other side. I tried to do this a number of times, but the shot only made her stop eating for a second and then would come the familiar tearing of flesh and crunching of bones. I gave it up in despair and she had a square meal. When she finally did go away she did it when I was not paying attention and did not see her. We supposed that she was the same lioness that tried the same trick the next night with Jack Terry but she was careless and finally crept up close to the little window in the *boma* to investigate and see what really was going on inside. When Jack looked out at the bait she snarled right in his face. Jack did not even bother to put the gun to his shoulder. The muzzle was resting on the opening of the window while the butt was on the ground. Jack's idea was to get the gun off as soon as possible — whether it hit her or not — just to get it off immediately. The result was that it actually went off right in her face. Again the shock must have been terrific. However, the bullet did not hit her square in the head but tore alongside the jaw and into the neck without hitting any vertebrae or other vital parts. Nor did it cut any big arteries or large veins causing her to bleed to death. At any rate, it did not kill her, and in the morning we had the hunt of our lives. Of course she turned up when least expected but did not get any of us and we all fired together in a couple of volleys which put her out of business."

Obviously, lions have grown much wiser in subsequent years. Today, even if it were legal to shoot from a *boma*, I am sure that any and all lions in the vicinity would be gone for the night after the first shot. HTF

Chapter 18

Crisis!

Another memorable incident took place during my father's safari in 1913. This was something that might have serious consequences even today, but which created a life-threatening crisis in those days at the beginning of our century. Unfortunately, his hunting diary mentions it only briefly and does not dwell on any details, so what follows is as I remember it, coming from his verbal account over 50 years ago.

After being on safari from early March to mid-June, during which several side-trips were made into and out of Nairobi, a catastrophic accident happened to George Outram. I would add, however, that after this crisis had passed, I think dad was probably secretly pleased to have been able to bring the safari and his professional hunter through it successfully. I say this, because I am convinced that he was a frustrated surgeon who had been pressured into entering the family business upon graduation from college two years earlier. But as events proved, he certainly had the opportunity of putting his layman's knowledge of medicine to work.

In 1913 safaris generally consisted of large caravans of porters, traveling on foot from camp to camp and from hunting area to hunting area. Compared to the later motorized hunts, the benefits and handicaps of the foot safari were mixed. Of course, prior to World War I there was vastly more game in East Africa than in the latter part of the 20th century. The problem was that whereas now one can cover hundreds of miles in a relatively short time, in those days all travel was on foot, so the area covered was inevitably somewhat limited.

It was on one of those treks that disaster struck, something that should never have happened. Somehow, a gun bearer tripped, and as he stumbled, the rifle he was carrying went off. I cannot believe that the gun bearer of those days was taught to carry a firearm with a cartridge in the chamber, much less with the safety off. But in any case, a .470 discharged, sending a 500-grain bullet crashing into and through Outram's right leg just below the knee. It shattered both the tibia and fibula, but fortunately did not cut any artery, or he would have bled to death then and there. However, there he was — totally immobilized and over 100 miles from any hospital.

The first thing my father — the frustrated surgeon — did was to pour a whole bottle of bichlorate of mercury into the wound of the badly injured Outram, who by then had gone into shock. One might think that such an incredible treatment would have done the patient in, but apparently it did what it was meant to do, because as it turned out no infection developed, and Outram lived to tell the tale. However, the bones in his leg were fused, and he walked with a limp for the rest of his life.

The next step was to organize the somewhat demoralized porters. Their white hunter had been shot, and they were sure he would die. But my father, *bwana m'kubwa*, as they called him, was a born linguist who had quickly picked up the "kitchen" Swahili of the day, took over the direction of the safari. Despite desertions by some, a litter was built and teams of porters were organized for what must have been a frightfully painful ordeal for Outram. Then it then took several days to carry him to Fort Hall, where there was a hospital to be found.

Eventually, he was ensconced under the skilled care of Sister Spenser, a nurse who was working on the very primitive edge of civilization. Initially, from time to time he was apparently delirious, so one night when he cried out in alarm, Miss Spenser assumed he was again hallucinating. He claimed he had seen a leopard standing outside his open window with its paws on the sill, peering in on the helpless and very alarmed patient — it would only have taken one very easy leap. The incident was passed off as delirium until the next morning, when upon his insistence, the nurse and staff trekked outside only to discover the footprints of a very large tom leopard right where the "delirious" Outram had insisted he had seen one watching him. Things were indeed somewhat different in those days when a leopard was able to peer in a hospital window.

The 1913 safari, from left: Lyman Hine, the legendary George Outram, and Jack Terry.

Another photo of George Outram, my father's PH in 1913.

In the meanwhile, dad, whose hunting companions had set off for their return to America, realized that Outram's recovery from the gunshot was assured and that he was clearly out of danger. So he proceeded to put a couple of small safaris together. He hunted unsuccessfully for sable in the Shimba hills near the coast and then for buffalo and rhino with considerably more success on various private farmlands in the Nairobi area.

While the hunting itself throughout the long safari was something he would never forget, the frustrated surgeon also had the greater satisfaction of having saved a remarkable man's life.

The reader might be interested in a postscript to this incident with George Outram. He must have been one of those men with the "bark still on" as my grandfather's close friend and hunting companion, the artist Frederick Remington, used to call the old trappers and frontiersmen of our American west. Outram, an immigrant from Australia, had fought his way through the Boer war, and in later years was a major in the British forces in East Africa during World War I. Between those two wars he had become one of the early professional hunters in Kenya, but all this came to an end when he was fatally mauled by a lioness at Taveta in 1922.

Outram may well have been a tough *hombre*, but he was not a good shot. It has been written elsewhere that on that fatal day he was mauled while saving his client's life. However, that is not quite what happened. Actually, his client had only wounded the lioness, which then charged. Outram tried to stop her with his big double, but either missed entirely or at best inflicted a non-stopping wound, whereupon she grabbed him by the abdomen and carried him off into the brush. In justice to what must have been a badly shaken client, it took a great deal of courage for him to follow Outram's shouts and run after the wounded lioness, finally finishing her off with a heart shot, but this he did. Sadly, however, George Outram died two days later in Mombasa from peritonitis.

Chapter 19

Simba!

Having told one sad tale of my lost elephant, I must recount another failure of sorts — this time about a lion that certainly scared several years off my life and might well have terminated it then and there.

Phyllis, Tami Miglio, the two trackers, and I were crowded into John Northcote's hunting car on our 1987 safari in Botswana. At the time we were camped at King's Pool on the Chobe River. Of all the camps where I have stayed on various safaris, none is as exquisitely beautiful as this place. We even had our own private hippo — Horace, as we called him — living in the pool a few yards from where we gathered each evening for sundowners and tall tales.

Dave Ommanney had driven to Kasane to renew his visa and would be gone for another day, so John was handling all of us. We had been out for a couple of hours, working northwest from our camp, when there was an urgent tap on the car roof. John stopped immediately. I grabbed my rifle off the rack, got out of the car, and was ready — but for what I did not know. Apparently, the trackers had spotted a large ginger-maned lion. During this safari we had seen quite a few lionesses, but precious few males. However, a few days earlier John, Dave and I had barely missed out on a beautiful black-maned fellow after we had tracked him through the Botswana dust for about three hours. When we finally caught up with the cat and his lady friend, they was sleeping it off under a tree, unseen by us. We first spotted the lioness, but she had already seen us and was off like a shot. The old boy woke up and realized that something was wrong — or that he was about to lose the love of his life — so he took off after her. I never got a shot, and because we had left the girls back in the car, we had to call it quits and return. That had been a big disappointment.

But hope springs eternal, and this time I had great expectations. I

Botswana. On the track of another lion. From left: Dave Ommanney, John Northcote, the author and the tracker.

still had not seen the lion, although I am told he was lying down watching us in pretty good view. Everyone else, even the girls, could see him. I simply was not looking in the right place. It was not until he got up and started to move out that I finally spotted him and only had time for a snap shot. I threw the rifle up and fired all in one motion. The lion dropped instantly with a growl. "Good shot!" John said as he pounded me on my back. But then the anticlimax: the trackers said he had gotten up almost immediately and run off. I still was not alarmed and was pretty sure we would find a dead lion 100 yards or so beyond.

He had been lying down with three or four females in a cluster of trees and brush, probably waiting in ambush for game. When I shot, the lionesses had cleared out without delay; I saw them go. But when we reached the spot where I had hit the male, we found where he had dropped and had then clawed the dusty earth in a frantic and successful effort to regain its feet and run. We followed the tracks across a few hundred yards of open grasslands and into another thick growth of trees and heavy underbrush. We found some blood, but very little. He obviously had not been hit in the lungs, for the blood was not frothy, and if I had found his heart, he would have been dead before he ever reached the second thicket. At the same time we reasoned that he could not have been gut shot, or he would not have dropped the way he did. The only conclusion John could reach was that my shot — as often happens when you fire too quickly — had gone high, grazing the spine and momentarily paralyzing him. Thus the lion dropped, but only for a few seconds until recovering the use of his legs and could get up and run. Had my shot gone one inch lower, it would have broken his back, or if lower still, it would have smashed one if not both shoulders and probably have caught the lungs as well. But those are "ifs." The point is: We had a wounded lion on our hands. What could we do?

The thick brush into which he had obviously run was a sort of island in the middle of some grassy plains. So the first thing was to drive around, looking for blood or some evidence that he had been badly hurt. Seeing nothing and returning to our starting point, John rightly insisted that we should not go after the lion, while leaving the girls alone in the car. There was no choice but to take them back to camp and then return to the scene of action.

The round trip was made in just a little over an hour. John was perfectly happy with this, because it is always good to wait a while after wounding a dangerous animal. This gives it time to die or at least to lie down and stiffen up.

When we resumed the hunt, we pondered over the best course of action, and decided to drive around the trees once more. This time we found some tracks going out. So we concluded that our original conjecture had been right: I had nicked the top of his spine. But having nothing worse than a pretty sore back, he had recovered sufficiently to leave with the females. We obviously were not going to catch up with him, so there was nothing to do but admit failure and quit. We were pretty confident that he had not been badly hurt and would recover completely.

We spent the rest of the day looking for buffalo, greater kudu, or anything else that might come along. Having no success, we started

Dave supervising the building of a machan for lion hunting. (The lions came, but there was not a worthwhile trophy in the group.)

back to camp in the late afternoon and on the way came to the scene of our morning adventure. John was curious to find out just what the lion had done, so we stopped to investigate. We walked into the brush, looking for tracks in the hope that we would be able to see where he had been and just where the lion and his lady friends had left. The

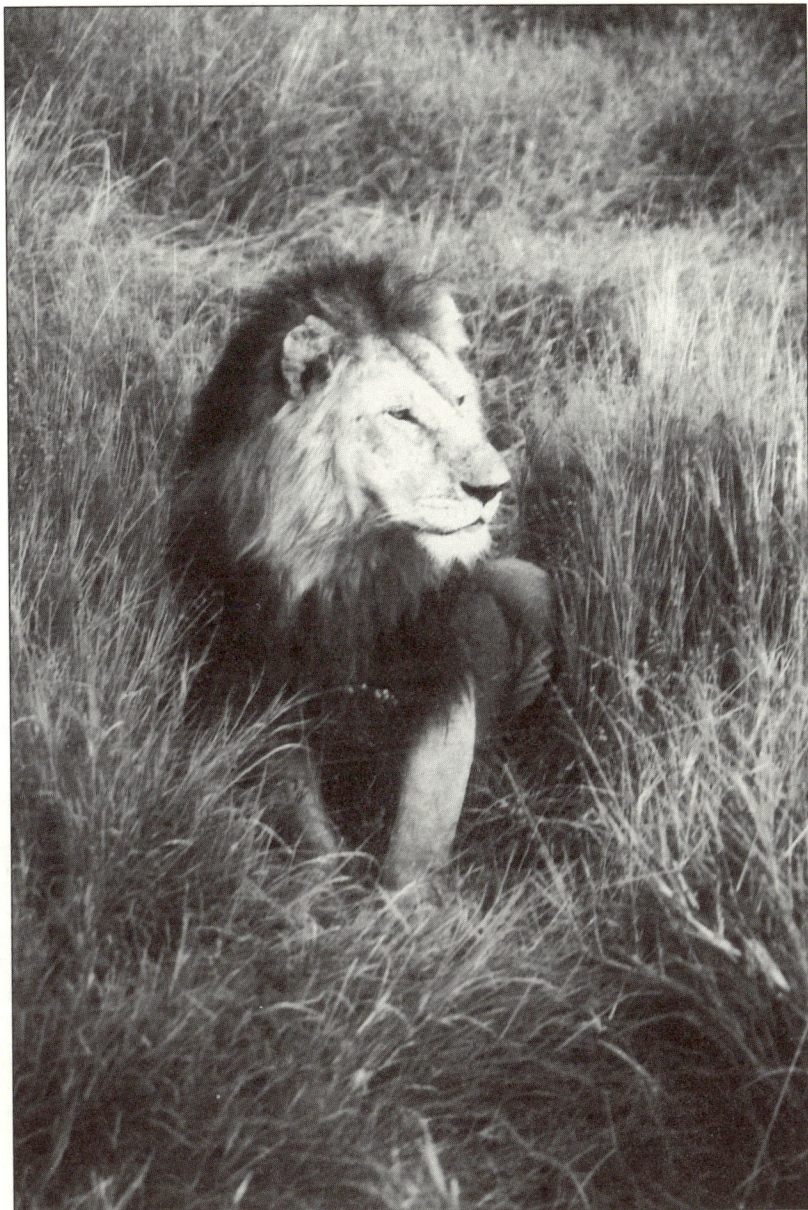

Where are those big girls with my supper? (And where was he when Dave and I were in the machan?)

sun was beginning to sink lower, so we did not have that much time. John just wanted to take a quick look; that was all.

We started in casually with John leading, followed by me, and then the two trackers. Out of habit I was carrying my rifle — the .300 magnum — but no one else was armed. Why bother? We were just making a quick check. We had not gone 50 feet into the brush when we heard a growl. Anyone who has ever heard the growl of an angry lion from a few yards away will never forget the sound. There were various reactions on our parts: John hurriedly backed off; I threw the safety off my rifle and raised it for whatever might happen; the boys simply disappeared. Then very slowly John and I retreated. My heart was in my mouth. We knew we were *very* close to a wounded lion. After what seemed forever, we made the clearing and the relative safety of the truck, where we found the trackers.

So the lion had not left after all. He was still there — how badly hurt we did not know. Obviously, we now had a very serious problem, because a wounded lion in the bush is a terribly dangerous animal. When hunting or tracking any dangerous game that has been wounded, the normal rules of sportsmanship are laid aside for the sake of safety. You get it any way you can. So first we tried to smoke him out. We lit a fire to windward of where we had heard him, but even with the terrible drought through which Botswana had been suffering, we were not able to get a fire really going or make enough smoke to have any effect. The only alternative was to go in and try to find him. To do this we would use the car as much as possible.

John loaded his shotgun with buckshot — the gun that would fail later — and climbed into the back of the truck with me. I had Dave's .458 with softs, and John passed his own .458 to one of the trackers and directed the other to drive — with the windows shut. In we went, but almost immediately it became apparent that the tracker had not had enough experience behind a wheel to handle the truck in this very thick brush. So he and John switched positions. The latter took his shotgun into the cab with him, leaving me in the back of the truck with one tracker still armed with the .458 and now the other with the .300 (I had no idea whether they could shoot or not). Then we were off again.

I have to admit I was scared. We had recently heard of a safari in the immediate neighborhood that had the disconcerting experience of a wounded lion springing into the back of the truck amidst the client and trackers. Having an angry lion in such close proximity really clears the air. A wild melee and a lot of frantic scrambling followed by shots going off in every direction. Miraculously no one was hurt, and the lion was finally dispatched when the professional jumped from the cab and finished him off. I certainly did not relish the thought of a similar experience and felt awfully naked, sitting up there, making a wonderful target upon which a hurt, angry and vengeful lion could easily leap.

It was hard going, even with the truck in low range four wheel drive, and at any instant I expected to see the lion charge, or worse still, feel him land on my back. However, he had obviously moved, because there was no sign of him where we had heard the growl. It was not long, however, before we began to find the lionesses; apparently, they had not left either and were evidently right there in the brush with him. They did not bother us, however, nor did we get any closer than we could help. But there was still no sign of the male.

Eventually, John gave up in disgust and drove out. We would have to go in on foot — he and I would; the trackers refused. There were those striking trackers again, but this time one could hardly blame them. Without question this developed into the most frightening experience of my life. Visibility was much worse than it had been from the elevated platform in the truck. We could only work our way ahead very slowly, and very carefully, and it was impossible to see more than a few yards in front of us. After all I had read and heard about wounded lions in the brush, I could not imagine how we would ever stop a determined charge if he came for us from 10 — 20 feet.

When it began to get really dark, we had no choice but to quit for the night. By then I was ready to go. My hands were sweaty, my knees weak, and my pulse must have been going at least 150 beats a minute. So it was with a sigh of relief and no objections whatever from me that we finally returned to the truck and started back to camp and a badly needed martini — maybe even two.

By the time we set out again the next morning before daylight, Dave had gotten back from Kasane and joined in our search — the more eyes and guns the better. However, John was fairly confident that we would find a dead lion. He reasoned that because he had not left the brush during the previous day, he was more seriously hurt than we had thought and probably had died during the night. This time the boys went in with us, which was reassuring to me, because it meant that they did not expect to find a living lion either. We searched for at least an hour — every yard of underbrush and trees. However, there was no sign of either lion or lionesses. From a very small pool of blood, we found where he had been lying when he growled at us, just about 30 feet from the spot where John and I had been standing. John was very surprised that he had not charged us when we were that close. We then found several tracks, and eventually saw where they had cleared out completely. John reasoned — correctly, I am sure — that the lion had left immediately after growling at us, or we would have found him one way or another the previous evening. The lionesses obviously had gone sometime during the night.

Our original reconstruction of a slightly wounded lion subsequently proved to be correct. Another safari that we ran into a few days later reported seeing a large ginger-maned lion in the area where we had been hunting. He was walking somewhat stiffly, but was obviously not crippled in any way. They were not after lion, so they let him go. Almost certainly this was the same one that had nearly scared the life out of me. I was relieved, because we were now sure he would recover completely and that his roars would soon be heard again in the African night — but hopefully not his growl from 30 feet away in the thick brush.

Chapter 20

Lo, the Poor Baboon!

Baboons are funny people. Unlike such serious researchers as George Schaller, the late Dian Fosse, Hugo Van Lawick and Jane Goodall, I have never made a scientific study of any wild animals — or any domestic ones either, for that matter. But I have always been intrigued by baboons, probably because they are the only primates other than man with which I have had any particular contact. There are lots of monkeys in Africa, but they are usually pretty well concealed in the treetops, or else they allow only a fleeting glimpse as they swing away to wherever monkeys go. But baboons are much more visible, and can provide diversion and enjoyment for a safari client.

Several instances come to mind. Once when Phyllis and I were having lunch at Keekorok Lodge in the Mara, we heard a shriek from the other end of the dining patio. Apparently, some brazen baboon had leaped upon the table and snatched a dinner roll right out of the hand of some female tourist. Then it was off across the lawn like a shot with various waiters in hot pursuit. Needless to say neither baboons nor waiters are so brazen in the wild.

A few years later, we were back in the Mara — this time at Serena Lodge — and were warned to keep our windows and doors shut. If we did not, presently we might well see some baboon sitting in a nearby tree, fondling my Pentax camera or draping my wife's necklace around its neck. We followed this good advice and had no trouble. However, not far from our room, one was sitting on the railing, and we could tell it was just waiting to see whether we closed the door or not; we did.

Another time John Northcote and I were hunting in the Botswana bush country. The afternoon was wearing on, and as dusk approached, we decided to sit until dark at a promising spot by the Chobe River in the hope that a kudu or some buffalo might come to drink. I had chosen an especially high anthill on which to wait, because it afforded a good view over 360 degrees and for a good distance as well. I assumed that if I sat very still, any animal coming for water would think I was just an extension of the anthill. Such was not the case, however.

I had noticed quite a few droppings when I clambered up on it; they were very human in appearance, but I knew that couldn't be the case. Presently I heard the answer. I certainly was not hidden from view, because across the clearing and from the safety of the forest a baboon was making a terrible scene, barking incessantly and angrily. It carried on until we finally left at sundown. Apparently, all this fuss had been because I was sitting on its anthill, and it was letting me know this in no uncertain terms. Baboons are funny people — or are they really that different from the rest of us?

Perhaps the most interesting experience I had with them was a tragicomic confrontation between man, baboon, and lion that took place later on that same safari. It was just after our futile search for the slightly wounded ginger-maned lion. After we returned the next day and when it had become apparent beyond any doubt that the lions had cleared out, John, Dave, and I paused to think what we should do next.

The trackers called our attention to an awful racket in a small forest across the clearing. It was obviously caused by a pack of very angry baboons. They were barking like mad and making a great to-do. John and Dave knew this could mean only one thing: They had been treed by a cat — leopard or lion — and were screaming their defiance from the safety of the heights. They reasoned that most likely it was a lion or lions, because leopards can climb as well as baboons, and if it were *chui*, the baboons would have taken off in frantic flight, rather than simply venting their wrath. We also wondered whether this just might be the lion and its pride that had been giving us so much trouble, so we decided to have a look.

It did not take long to get across the clearing and into the trees. Once there we moved very cautiously, because we knew big cats were about, and just maybe a wounded and angry lion was among them. The wind was in our favor, and the going was tolerably quiet, so we were able to get very close to the cause of all this noise. Presently, we

Come out, come out — wherever you are.

saw five lions in the underbrush not more than 30 or 40 yards away, but thankfully they had no idea we were there. One glance told us that this was not the same group as before; there were three females and two immature males, but no big ginger fellow. The lions did not see us, but the baboons did, and now they had a problem.

Over the years these intelligent animals have learned that they must always leave the trees when humans approach. They will flee to the safety of the heights if threatened by other animals, but not in the case of man, because then they are trapped and can easily be shot either by rifle or bow and arrow. So when they are in the trees and see people coming, they invariably come down with remarkable speed and scramble off to safety. But this time the baboons were in a dilemma.

We could see the indecision on their faces. They had stopped hollering and were rather frantically contemplating our approach. Normally this would have called for a rapid descent and subsequent flight on foot. But they also knew there were lions down below. First they looked at us, and then at them — what to do?

Finally, one big dog baboon's fear of man proved greater than his fear and hatred of cats and decided to make a break. He came down the tree like a fireman down a greased pole and rocketed off the instant his feet touched the ground, but he never had a chance. In two bounds a lioness had him. It was all over in an instant. The baboon was killed outright and devoured by the lions within a minute or two. In all their growling and squabbling they still had not noticed us. Only after they had finished eating, did they finally see us and quickly take off.

Then to the inestimable relief of the baboons, so did we.

Chapter 21

"The Bird Is On the Wing"

In years gone by when people spoke of an African safari, it was generally assumed that they were talking about a hunting trip to Africa. Today this association of words is no longer automatically made. Many people — many tourists — take "safaris" now. College and university alumni associations plan such trips on a regular basis, and we see them advertised almost weekly in the Sunday newspapers. Of course, this is a legitimate use of the term, for the Swahili word "*Safari*" simply means "trip" or "journey." So when I speak to someone about having taken, or being about to take, an "African Safari" he is usually genuinely interested and a bit envious, for such trips are the "in" thing today. But then a shadow of doubt may pass over his brow and he anxiously asks, "With a *camera*, I hope!" He is generally dismayed when I reply, "No, I am going on a *hunting* safari," immediately, I am in trouble and must prepare to defend such a brutal pursuit; either that, or he will simply say, "Oh."

However, for me a "safari" *is* a hunting safari; at least the "*safari m'kubwa*" — the great safari — is. Anything less is "*safari kidogo*" — the little safari. Nonetheless, I would be pretty narrow minded to insist that big game hunting is the only legitimate goal on a safari. Many sportsmen go on bird shooting or fishing safaris, and this was even true some years ago. Of course, there were and still are people who go into the bush armed primarily with the camera. For me it would be mighty expensive bird shooting or fishing if that were the only reason one went to Africa. While I have never done any fishing over there, I confess that to mix in a bit of wing shooting during a "regular" big game hunting safari is a wonderful change of pace. And as far as photography is concerned, over the years I have taken hundreds of slides and more recently hours of videos. Until recently I have always started off with tours in the game parks and preserves, because that is where you get the best game pictures — the ones that make non-hunters go "ooh" and "ah."

Even when hunting big game, it is always pleasant to break the routine a bit with some bird shooting, and a good francolin or guinea fowl curry is a welcome change from the usual high protein red meat fare. When the opportunity presents itself, I happily turn to the bird on the wing.

While it is sadly true that big game hunting in Africa is not what it used to be, this certainly is not true of bird shooting, which is still extraordinary. One wonderful aspect of it is that you do not need a dog. In fact, if you take one with you it will probably get bitten by a tsetse fly and die. However, dogs are really unnecessary. There are multitudes of birds for the asking: francolin, guinea fowl, doves of all sorts, several varieties of geese and best of all sand grouse. For all I know there are more species as well. Although I have never tried my hand at geese in Africa, the others have all provided me with ample — and quite humbling — sport.

Most of the time when a change of diet is desired, francolin or guinea fowl are simply shot with a .22 — through the head by Dave Ommanney, or generally either missed or through the body by me. I might add that guinea fowl especially are reluctant to fly, but can run like the wind, so they can be very hard to hit. Depending on how badly hurt it is, a man often cannot catch a crippled guinea fowl on foot. But when we wanted a change of hunting sport as well as diet, we often went after birds on the wing with the shotgun.

Back when I started hunting in Africa I considered myself a pretty fair clay bird shot. In fact, in those days I was often top gun in the club to which I belonged. However, by happenstance I have not done a whole lot of live bird shooting — much as I would like to. Consequently, when I started shooting at birds *on the wing* in Africa, I was in for a shock and an education. The first time was easy. I had been recovering from an attack of the stomach bug and was tired of convalescing around camp. At the time Dave was hunting with my two sons, so I went out looking for birds by myself. Within five minutes I put up a francolin, a bird somewhat the size of a ruffed grouse. Beginner's luck: I dropped it right away with one shot. "Why there's nothing to this," I said to myself; little did I know.

A few days later Dave suggested some sand grouse shooting. This is a truly wonderful bird. It is a little larger than our quail, but it reminds me a lot of our bobwhite, somewhat similar in appearance, and *very* much like it on the wing — flying like the wind. While you do occasionally see sand grouse out on the plains during the day, the usual way to hunt them with a shotgun is either the first thing in the morning or the last thing in the afternoon; these are the two times when they come in for water. If you park yourself by a water hole and wait for them to appear, you will soon be in for an exciting time. In fact, your gun barrel will not cool off as one after another rockets in for a drink. After watching me for a while, Dave commented that henceforth if he saw anything but either the lead bird or the tailender fall, he would know that I was shooting into the flock, and that would not be *comme il faut*. This cramped my style a bit, but apparently it is an unwritten but inviolate rule in British wing shooting. Shortly thereafter, he made one of the most extraordinary wing shots I had ever witnessed. There was a single way up high; I thought it was out of shotgun range, but apparently Dave did not. When he fired, the bird started down like a crippled World War I fighter, describing great circles in the air; all it needed was a trail of black smoke to complete the illusion of one of the Red Baron's victims falling from the sky.

My two sons were on that safari. While they had both been introduced to a bit of target shooting, neither one had ever fired anything larger than a .22 before our trip. Randy took to the high powered rifle with ease when he dropped an impala with one shot on the first day. And even Henry, my photographic son who had not intended to do any shooting, eventually heard the horn of the hunter and managed a zebra and a buffalo before the safari was over. But neither of them had ever fired a shotgun. To my amazement, they took to it like ducks to water — if the reader will pardon my simile in this context. My reaction was one of mixed pride and embarrassment, because both of them killed more birds that I — the great club champion. I managed to hit a few, but my sons really covered themselves with glory. How thrilling it was to see a flock coming at early light and to hear the whistling of their wings. And how we enjoyed our meal that night.

One other incident took place years later with Dave and John Northcote on the Chobe River in Botswana. This time we were after doves. They also fly in for water at the end of the day. So one evening the three of us ventured forth, full of confidence and three boxes of 12-gauge shells. Again, I blasted a bird on my first try — not a bad shot, I might add. Then we were somewhat disconcerted when John's shotgun misfired and subsequently would not fire at all. This happened *after* tracking the wounded lion in thick brush described in the earlier chapter and *after* checking my downed leopard with John carrying that same shotgun. I shudder to think what would have happened if he had needed to fire it at such a moment of crisis. In any case, John's bird shooting was done for the safari, but Dave and I carried on. Candidly, I had never shot doves before, so it certainly was a new and trying experience. Those little birds *never* fly in a straight line and *always* veer off just as the shooter is pulling the trigger. In any case, I got a few, but missed far more than I hit. On that occasion at least Dave did not do any great shakes either. Between the two of us we used up 75 shells and rather sheepishly returned to camp with only 15 birds. It was a humbling experience, and the next day we were back at the far less difficult task of hunting lions and buffalo.

Chapter 22

An End Run For A TD

The African animal I most admire and desire — one with which I have had little success — has to be the lion. I recounted earlier one successful encounter with *Simba* and one unsuccessful one, but sadly I have never gotten one of those MGM fellows with the big bushy manes. I have come close a couple of times, even passing up several males seen from a machan or blind, but I have never quite connected with a really good one.

But having given the lion its due, a close second in my order of priorities has to be either the elephant or Cape buffalo, and because I have never gotten the former and almost certainly never will, I turn here to the latter. *Mbogo* has always held a fascination for me. I am afraid of buffalo, because when finally provoked into aggressive action, it is in my opinion the most dangerous of the Big Five. And while I have eight buffalo to my credit, I have usually had trouble getting them. But I never shot a really big one; in fact, since Rowland Ward eliminated the measurement on the curl as a qualification my listings dropped off — 43½ inches being my largest spread. To make matters worse, I have usually had trouble making a clean kill. I managed well enough on my first buffalo — a cow for my son's leopard bait — on the next four I needed help from the professional's rifle. I did finally get one with one shot and without any trouble in 1987. It was my second on that trip, and while its horns are not that great — 40 inches — because it was the first bull I had shot cleanly and without help, I have them hanging inside the entrance to our house. Then in 1993 I managed another "solo" on the first of two buffalo, although I needed Dave's help when it came to the second. But it was on the first one shot with help during a 1987 Botswana safari that we scored a TD with an "end run."

We were with John Northcote. Even though the reader has met John earlier in this book, I should say something more about this bearded professional from Zimbabwe. After a long hitch in the Royal Navy during World War II (at which time he grew a massive beard that he has worn ever since), John eventually became a very successful professional hunter in East Africa. In time he got into the rather distasteful job of game control in which it is necessary to reduce the size of herds, taking males, females and even young. Then with the advent of Idi Amin and the closing down of hunting in Uganda where he was at the time, he was forced to look elsewhere. He moved to what was then Rhodesia, now Zimbabwe, and resumed his chosen profession taking clients on safari. Eventually, he also took this up in Botswana, where we hunted with him in 1987.

He was 67 years old at that time, but he acted like a man in his early 50s. John has legs like Abraham Lincoln's, a long way from top to bottom. Consequently, he moves along effortlessly mile after mile, while his client — at least this client — sweats and gasps, trying to keep up. To my knowledge nowhere is this more evident than in hunting or pursuing buffalo.

One morning midway through our trip, John, Dave Ommanncy, and I were exploring the banks of the Chobe, hoping to find buffalo tracks made the night before. We knew there was a herd in the area, because we had already stalked it a couple of times, on each occasion having it spooked at the last minute by zebra that had spotted us. It is funny about those striped mules: when you are hunting them for lion or leopard bait, you sometimes will go all day without even seeing one, but stalk some trophy animal like the buffalo, and they seem to turn up at just the wrong moment every time. In any case this morning we hoped to pick up that herd again. We did not have long to wait.

No sooner had we gotten to the river, when we found fresh tracks along its bank and then heard the distinctive grunting of a herd of buffalo. Apparently, they had been drinking and were just then returning to the safety of the mopane some miles from the river. Right away, we were after them.

As I recall, John was in the lead with his trackers, then I, and finally Dave. We had not gone 300 yards before we caught sight of

The author and his southern Cape buffalo (Botswana, 1987).

their black shapes, moving slowly through the trees. After following them for a while without being detected, but also without being able to get into position for any kind of shot at a decent bull — if there was a decent one there — we realized that we had a problem. It is very difficult to catch up to a herd of buffalo, and even if you do, unless they are out in the open, all you generally see are the rear animals, and you are very apt to miss a good one that may be further up within the bunch. From the way they were headed, across the wind, we decided to try an "end run" around the herd on their downwind flank. So we took off — or rather John took off with the rest of us trying to keep up.

We had tried this same tactic with some buffalo a few days before — with an interesting result — interesting, to say the least. That morning John and I had been following on the track of a herd for some time when he decided to try to work our way around it. We set out, always keeping downwind. They were in the open, and we were moving parallel, keeping out of sight just inside the edge of some woods. Presently, the herd appeared right in front of us, and we froze. Not 10 yards away a young bull was standing still, staring right at me. He could not smell me, and I did not move a muscle. Apparently, while *mbogo* has excellent eyesight, he was having trouble making out some absolutely stationary people standing among some trees. We did not move, nor did the buffalo. He just stood there staring at me for at least five minutes, not knowing what I was. My fear was that he might decide to move closer for a better look; how close could I let him get without being forced to risk a shot? I could not even turn to look at John for direction. At just the critical moment, he seemed to be satisfied and lost interest. I breathed a sigh of relief as he then wandered off with the rest of the herd, that was still completely oblivious of our presence. Then, as usual, some zebra spotted us, sounded an alarm, and the buffalo were off in a panic. That concluded our attempt at an end run that day.

Now, back to our later attempt: I was in pretty fair shape for a man my age. In prep school and college I had been a varsity athlete. Since then I have been an avid mountain hiker and until fairly recently a technical alpine climber as well. But it was hard for me to believe that anyone, regardless of age, could move as quickly and quietly through the brush as John was doing without scaring off everything within 10 miles. However, he managed, and somehow the rest of us were able to keep up with this "elderly" professional.

On several occasions we drew up beside the herd, but each time they moved on before we could get a decent look. At this point John and Dave made an educated guess as to where they were heading, and we virtually sprinted around, racing to "cut them off at the pass" — and we won. We got to the top of a little hill that had pretty open woods all around it and then sat and waited. Had we guessed right, or had the herd arbitrarily branched off in some other direction, perhaps even crossing our track and picking up the dreaded scent of man? As far as we knew up to this point they were oblivious of our presence.

It is one thing to still-hunt, to sit and wait for a buck deer or some other animal possibly to happen along. When you know there are animals in the vicinity, and you hope that they are heading in your direction, it adds a new dimension to the excitement. It was not long before our work was rewarded. Almost as if by direction the buffalo appeared, coming right toward us, and it was obvious that if they continued on their course, they were bound to pass within 100 yards — and in the open.

I know my pulse was pounding, because I had never experienced anything quite like this with a herd of animals coming in our direction without knowing we even existed. Then the vagaries of hunting intervened. For some reason, they stopped and started halfhearted feeding. However, it was not all bad, because right up front there was a fairly good bull, certainly the best we could spot in the herd and even the largest we had seen thus far on the safari. He was standing broadside in some brush, but a shot seemed feasible. It was certainly worth a try, because up to this point we had not been having much success in finding trophies.

I was carrying Dave's .458 magnum with a soft point in the chamber, backed up with two solids. Even though it is a superb rifle for heavy and dangerous game, I am not wild about the .458, because it is just a bit too much. I have great trouble with flinching when I shoot it, and flinch I did this time. I fired twice, and it was obvious that I had hit the buff both times, but he wheeled and started off with the rest of the herd without difficulty. We knew right away that I had gut shot him — bad news with buffalo.

We took off, trying to catch up with them. This is not an easy thing to do when buffalo are spooked. Because I could not tell one from another, I was very pessimistic about ever finding this particular animal again. However, before long we did catch sight of them — obviously they had not been badly frightened — and wonder of wonders, the wounded bull was right there in front of us. Both John and Dave spotted him from some rather distinctive mark on his face. Again, he was standing broadside at about 100 yards; again I fired low on the shoulder. Again he took off, crossing directly in front of us. At this critical moment my rifle jammed as I was trying to pump another cartridge into the chamber. In anguished frustration I called out, "The gun's jammed!" whereupon both John and Dave fired as my bull was heading for thick cover. All was well, however, because very soon we heard that mournful moan which always signals a downed and dying buffalo. Indeed he was stone dead when we reached him.

The postmortem revealed all. My first shots had both hit, and one of them would ultimately have been fatal, but was too far back. There were also two unmistakable .458 holes within a couple of inches of each other on his shoulder. One was obviously my last shot, and the other was John's (who was also using a .458). But there was no sign of anything from Dave's .300 magnum. Then he rather sheepishly admitted that he had shot into an intervening tree as the buffalo ran by. But all's well that ends well, as the saying goes.

This had been an interesting and exciting hunt, one that I will not soon forget. Generally, I do not mount or take home a trophy that another person has also hit. But in this case my conscience did not bother me, because my first and third shots were all that was needed. John's turned out to have been only insurance, so that buffalo now hangs on my wall as a shoulder mount. All of us had certainly gotten our exercise that day, and to boot, we had scored a TD on an end run.

Chapter 23

The Year of the Buffalo

The Chinese have a traditional way of identifying the years in the cycle of their calendar: The Year of the Rabbit, the Year of the Rat, or the Year of the Dragon, etc. As far as my African hunting is concerned, 1993 was "The Year of the Buffalo."

At the time I was pretty sure that this was also the year of my last safari. I had said this after each of my previous trips, and it had never turned out to be true. But I was getting older with more and more aches and pains, weakened knees, eyesight that was not what it had been 20 years before, and deafness that made my long-suffering professional almost have to shout at me to take the one second from the left or perhaps not to shoot. Often as not, the animal heard it before I did and departed post haste. It seemed time to quit. Obviously, it was not, but I really thought so at the time.

This sentimental safari, once again taken with Dave Ommanney as my professional, was especially welcome, because it meant a return to the area of my first love — where my African hunting had started — Tanzania. But it was different in at least three respects: First, this time we hunted neither on the Kisigo in central Tanzania nor at Maswa near the Victoria *Nyanza*, but instead on the Masai Steppe in southern Masailand; second, I was alone on this trip; and third, the game was noticeably depleted from what it had been in 1971. However, while this is true, there certainly was no shortage of buffalo. We saw buffalo, day after day, by the hundreds if not the thousands, and although I had shot them previously — some better than others — I had never gotten one with at least a 46 inch spread in order to qualify for the record book. So this was one of my somewhat limited objectives this time around. Sadly, it was not to be. As far as I know that Big One will still be roaming the veldt for some time to come, but that is hardly to say I did not have a lot of excitement with *mbogo*.

A few days into the safari we had reports from some of the neighboring Masai that a great lion — *simba m'kubwa* with a huge mane — had killed three of their cattle. Of course, such marauders are *always* described as males with great manes, usually black manes at that. In this case, while we never found the lion per se, we did indeed see the tracks of a large male, so there may have been some truth to their report. In any case, as the afternoon was drawing to a close, I spotted a herd of buffalo grazing about a half a mile off to our left. This in itself was a rarity, because I almost never saw game before either the trackers or the professional. Dave checked quickly with his glasses to make sure they were not simply a herd of Masai cattle, and then said, "You done good!" — which compliment in itself made my day.

Riding in the vehicle, we were able to cut the distance about in half, but then we had to start stalking on foot, while always trying to keep trees or bushes between them and us. Eventually, we got to within a respectable range, probably a little over 100 yards. Dave could not find anything as large as I wanted, but he reminded me that I had three buffalo on my license and that we needed a bait. So I agreed to take a perfectly respectable male, standing off to the right of the herd. I fired a .375 solid at the middle of his shoulder. He jumped and started to run to the right, the direction in which he had been facing. However, the herd went off to the left, so he quickly reversed himself and followed after them. Then almost immediately, the whole troop stopped and stood facing us in something approaching a semicircle. We stopped. At this point we had lost sight of the bull I had fired at, and I was somewhat concerned. Then when they finally turned and ran off quite leisurely, we followed them, trying to keep out of sight as best we could.

We quickly got quite close, and Dave even spotted my bull among them when he saw one with blood on its nose, but he ran before I could shoot. A few minutes later, we found him still again, and this time he was separated from the herd that had finally run some distance away. The bull was obviously badly hurt, but even so he immediately took off to our left. I fired once, then again. With the last shot he appeared almost to be going down, but he recovered and disappeared into some very thick brush.

Another buffalo, this one also from Botswana in 1987.

I did not like this development at all. We had no idea just how badly off he was, and all of us were only too aware of the danger of going into the brush after a wounded buffalo. A buffalo can become perhaps the most dangerous animal on earth when hurt and angry — and we knew that this one had been badly hurt and, if still alive, was by now very angry. However, we had to look for him; that is part of the code, so we started by circling the quite large stretch of brush, moving very slowly. Dave warned me to keep watching behind, lest he charge from the rear, something buffalo do upon occasion. But there was no sign. Was he dead or simply waiting for the right moment to come for us? Finally, we realized we would have "to bite the bullet" and go into the brush after him. We moved very slowly and ever so carefully, holding our rifles at ready. From time to time a tracker would climb a tree in an effort to spot it, but then we would move on. Presently, when the tracker was again up a tree, there was a sudden relaxation of tension. When this happens, you are aware of it immediately. About 20 yards ahead we saw the buffalo — stone dead.

189

The rest can be summed up briefly. My first shot had hit right where I had aimed, in the middle of the shoulder. Why it did not break the shoulder is a mystery. Almost certainly a soft point would have performed the job better. But even so, it was an ultimately fatal shot. My second shot, fired when he was running, hit too far back, but the third one, a snap shot taken in desperation just as he was disappearing into the brush again, was perfect. This is the one at which he stumbled. The bullet smashed his shoulder and obviously put him down within a few yards. This was buffalo number one.

A few days later we were still looking for the Big One. We had been working around a very large herd most of the morning and then came on them again in the afternoon. These buffalo were distinctly nervous and jumpy. Try as we might, we just could not get really close to them, and yet we were confident that they were unaware of our presence; so we could only conclude that lions were hunting them as well. The trackers spread out in an attempt to find a way of getting to within decent viewing and shooting distance when one of them returned to say that he had heard a buffalo bellowing, which — if true — probably meant a lion had made a kill. Since a big lion was number one on my priority list, we immediately dropped the buffalo stalking and shifted our attention to locating the alleged cat.

Dave was leading, with me directly behind, followed by a tracker, the government game scout, and finally the second tracker. We had not gone very far when something happened awfully quickly. I saw Dave suddenly back-pedal furiously while throwing up his rifle and firing a shot from that big .470 double. I will never forget the great sheet of flame that spewed forth from the muzzle in the late afternoon light. A bull did a cartwheel just off to our left and crashed down. I did not react, but simply stood there with my mouth open, watching it struggle to rise. Dave yelled, "Shoot, Hank!" I finally awoke and proceeded to put a couple of shots into him with my .375 Magnum. These fairly flattened him, but still did not kill him outright. Dave fired another .470, and then I finished the job with one more from my rifle.

This had been an unprovoked and wholly unexpected charge, and probably only Dave's quick reaction saved one of us from being gored

190

or tossed. He shot for the brain and just missed, yet it had been close enough to drop the animal — something very difficult to do with buffalo — but then it had taken the most consummate amount of lead to end the struggle. These animals are so hard to kill if the first shot is not just right.

This was an old, but not large bull. It obviously had been a loner and definitely not part of the herd we had been stalking earlier. We had come into "his turf," and he wanted us out, so he came for us. This had been a rather dicey experience — at least for me. I did not want to keep the trophy, because I had neither been hunting it nor scored the first hit. However, it was not wasted. This bull was subsequently hung for bait at our lion blind.

These first two animals were bad enough, but not as frightening as the third. After all, while there was a lot of suspense with the first, and we did come up on him twice in the bush, still we were never that close to him, and then he was ultimately found dead — to our great relief. The second charged so quickly that we did not have time to be frightened. There was no suspense, only reflexive action on Dave's part. However, there was more than enough suspense and action with the third one.

The end of the safari was fast approaching, and even though we had hung baits in at least six locations, we had not seen a "hairy lion" on any of them. There were lionesses and cubs, and I had passed up a young male on bait. To our frustration we even found evidence of a good one having been there in the middle of the night. All this was in front of the blind we had built. The bait was pretty well gone, what with the lionesses, hyenas, and those two young males, working on it, so we decided to go after one more buffalo. Frankly, I was not wildly enthusiastic about this. I am a great believer in the law of averages, and believe that if you hunt dangerous game long enough, sooner or later one of them will get you. On various safaris I had already had my share of what I considered too close encounters with *mbogo*. However, I agreed to go after them once more. We hoped it would be the Big One I was after, but we had resolved to take any shootable male. I wanted that "hairy" lion to come back, and we needed a new bait if we were to have any chance of making that happen.

Quite late in the afternoon there was a tap on the roof of the car, signaling that a tracker had spotted something. What it turned out to be was a couple of bulls, grazing near the edge of the woods about a half mile away. We stopped and, checking the wind, began stalking. It was not hard going, because we did not have to struggle through any of those awful wait-a-bit thorns or heavy brush this time. Quite quickly we got up to within about 100 yards. By this time they were lying down and chewing their cud. Dave picked out the better of the two and told me to take him.

In all the time I have hunted big game in Africa, I have never really gotten used to shooting off a tripod. Actually, if used properly, it avoids a lot of missed or wounded game and is thus a much more humane way of hunting. I have done some good shooting off them, but I have also done some terrible shooting off them — like missing a roan standing broadside out in the open about 100 yards away. Consequently, if I can sit and shoot or, better still, aim from a prone position, I am much more confident. In this case the buffalo was lying down, quartering sharply away. It had to be a fairly tricky shot, requiring me to hit him fairly well back in the paunch with the bullet then travelling forward into the chest cavity. To do this, I elected to shoot from a sitting position. This was probably a mistake, because he was partially concealed by grass and perhaps also by thorn twigs. If I had shot standing up, not using the tripod, but instead a tree that was right next to me as a brace, I would have had a better angle and probably nailed him right then and there. However, all that is hindsight. The upshot was that I fired while sitting, and both buffalo leaped up and were off into the brush like rockets. I threw a desperation shot at my bull, but without much hope of hitting him. I could only say to myself, "Here we go again!" Why couldn't I simply drop one of these creatures out in the open on my first shot as I had once done in Botswana? In any case we moved into the brush with great caution. My shot had wounded the bull, and he was hurting and plenty angry.

It was not long before we caught sight of one of the bulls, running off to our left. The trackers were certain that this was the one I had shot at, so we followed it. Within five minutes, and after painstaking caution, we stopped and looked right into the face of a bull, standing not 15 yards away. To hit it accurately would be a formidable job, because my shot would have to go through all kinds of brush, and one simply does not know how a bullet is going to behave under those conditions. Don't *ever* believe any ammunition manufacturer or hunter, for that matter, who claims that such and such a cartridge is a good "brush cutter." There is no such animal. We all know that a light high velocity bullet will not go anywhere through brush, but sometimes we can be fooled by a heavy bullet that will pass through fairly thick stuff one time, but then be shattered by apparently the same sort of brush another. To illustrate this: Earlier in the safari I shot a very good lesser kudu at a bit over 200 yards. It went a short distance and then dropped dead. When we examined the kudu, its shoulder looked like it had been hit by buckshot; there were nine holes in it. Obviously, my bullet had hit a twig or something on the way. It could not have been much, because as far as I could tell at the time, I had had a long, but clear, shot. Fortunately, whatever it was must have been very close to the animal, or I never would have touched it and would have kicked myself for another bad shot. That would have been too bad, because this bull was an exceptional trophy that scored well into the record rook. But that bullet had absolutely disintegrated.

In another scenario a day or two later, I shot at a buffalo quite a way off (yes, still another one in this Year of the Buffalo). Obviously, I never touched it, and we investigated to see why. About half way up we found where my *soft nose* bullet had gone right through an eight-inch tree (and African wood is very hard), then traveled through a bunch of brush, and finally bounced intact off another tree when it was spent — all this in a *perfectly* straight line. Why, on one occasion, will a twig break up a heavy bullet when on another a tree will not even divert it? I do not know. The best policy is to avoid both if possible.

However, with this fellow in the bush I had no choice. So I aimed for the midsection and fired. Again, he whirled and crashed off. This time Dave said with some disgust that next time he would shoot first. In my emotionally weakened condition I raised no objection, so on we went, working along the track, which by then was showing some blood.

It was not long before we found him again, staring at us with that grim look only a buffalo can generate. He was standing — again in very thick brush — only 10 yards away, and it was clear he intended to flee no more. He raised his head and let out a grunt, which always signals a charge. Immediately, Dave shot. The buffalo crashed down, amidst much thrashing and bellowing. This time I needed no prodding and proceeded to fire two shots, reload my rifle, and fire two more. After all this cannonading, the poor fellow died. By now it was so late that we could do nothing. So we simply left him, hoping no lion or hyena would find him, and then wended our way back to camp. However, throughout our return Dave and I were both troubled, because each of us suspected that the boys had been wrong and that this was not the buffalo I had *originally* shot at out in the open. If this were true, it meant there was still a wounded animal somewhere out there with all those young Masai cattle herders around. This could be serious.

However, upon our return the next morning, to our inestimable relief, we found where my first shot had hit his back. The shot missed everything vital, but then I had made an ultimately fatal shot when I paunched him as he ran off. Ironically, I had held out no hope for that one, fired as he was disappearing into the woods. My third shot, the one taken when we first faced him in the brush, really was not all that bad. I did miss the brain, the bullet actually going through horn, but it was only an inch or two off — that brush again? Dave's shot had gone right up the animal's nose as it had raised its head, preparing to come for us, but again, the shot missed the brain. This did drop him, however, and the rest was simply a matter of burning a considerable amount of gunpowder, putting the bull out of its misery.

So this was the Year of the Buffalo. Unfortunately, even with a *fourth* one that had been given to us by the Masai after it had been killed by a lion, we still were not able to bring that big fellow with the long hair to bait. I can only conclude that these were very educated lions that had to contend with the Masai's poisoned baits. They would come once, but never again; having been poisoned and surviving, they learned not to go back to the well once too often.

Chapter 24

Rendezvous In the Bush

Some years prior to our antics with the buffalo described in the previous chapter, I experienced the most exciting moment in my African hunting — and almost the end of it.

In 1975 my wife, Phyllis, along with Ralph and Gunlog Millet, friends from Connecticut, went to Kenya on my second safari. KENYA: where it had all started. At the time we did not know that its glorious days of hunting since before the time of Theodore Roosevelt were about to end. Because of poaching, elephant hunting was for all practical purposes already closed, and within two more years everything would be shut down. So I really got in on the last scene of the last act of an unforgettable drama.

I had engaged David Ommanney again, and he decided to start us off on the Tana River in eastern Kenya. Our first camp was on the Ida-Sa-Godana cooperative ranch. Calling it a "ranch" does not imply that it was anything like South African game ranches. It was simply an unfenced cattle ranch with a lot of wild game.

On the very first afternoon we ran into a fair herd of 50 — 60 buffalo. Dave and I immediately left the others in the second car and started our stalk on foot. I was carrying a Remington Model 700, .375 magnum, with a soft in the chamber and two solids in the magazine. We worked up as close to the herd as possible, crawling on our hands and knees. All went well until I started to pay the price for wearing short pants — we were in and among those awful little thorn trees, When I couldn't stand it any longer, I cheated a bit by creeping in a low crouch. The buffalo, that had been watching these strange creatures out of curiosity, then immediately recognized us for what we were and ran. I assumed that was the end of it, but not long afterward we caught up with the herd again, and this time we managed

195

to get to within a couple of hundred yards. Glassing them carefully, Dave saw a pretty good bull. He was lying down in front, half facing us. However, he doubted whether I could deliver a fatal shot because of the angle at which the buffalo was lying. On the other hand I was pretty sure I could slip a bullet in just under the horn and ear, striking the neck near the point of the shoulder. Hopefully, it would then penetrate the chest cavity and leave one very dead buffalo. In addition, I was confident, because I was standing by a pretty substantial tree against which I could brace my rifle for the shot. I also felt secure in my shooting, because that very morning I had made a nice shot on a Peter's gazelle at about the same distance, and it presents a much smaller target than a buffalo. Without further ado I fired. I was certain I saw him lurch, but then as expected, he leaped up and ran off with the herd.

What was unexpected was Dave's reaction. He was furious, because he had been considering moving me around for a slightly better angle. He knew that from where we were it would be a delicate shot at best. And since I had not always covered myself with glory on our first trip, he was debating whether it would not be wise to risk a move, hoping for a better angle from which to shoot. In any case I had fired.

Not expecting the report of a .375 magnum to go off right next to his ear, he had jumped and consequently momentarily lost sight of the buffalo in his glasses. He did not know whether I had hit it or not. However, Mutambuki, our tracker, was sure I had. At this point I was not concerned, because I *knew* I had shot well and had struck right where I had aimed — on the point of the shoulder. I fully expected to find a dead buffalo not far off.

But we did not, and even after following the spoor for perhaps a half a mile, there still was no sign, and we could find no trace of blood. Then I did begin to have doubts — perhaps I had not really seen it flinch when I fired — and by now Dave was sure *I* was the one who had flinched and thus had missed.

Then to my great relief we came up on the herd again. Obviously, they had not been very alarmed by the one shot, and to add insult to injury there was my bull, placidly grazing out front. Presently he raised

Young Masai tending cattle.

his head and looked right at us. For the second time I had a good tree to lean against, and this time Dave told me to let loose. When I did, I was again pretty sure that he lurched or stumbled, but whether he did or not, he turned and ran off with the herd. It would be a long running shot, but I fired a third time, and then they were gone, leaving only the proverbial cloud of dust to show where they had been.

Dave thought the first of these latter two shots had gone low, because he had seen what appeared to be dust jump under the buffalo, but worse still, he thought he had seen a running calf slump when I fired my third shot. By then I was completely confused and demoralized. After starting off so confidently, my nerves were pretty well shattered. The first shot had felt so good; so had the second. I was not holding out any real hope for the third, that had been taken at a running target at an increasingly long range, but why had that third shot even been necessary? In any event we set off in pursuit and followed the herd's track fruitlessly until dark.

Our ride back to camp was a bit strained to say the least. Dave was still fuming over my having fired the first shot when I did, but I was upset too. My pride was damaged, and I simply could not understand how I had missed. Apparently I had, but unless my sights were off, I *knew* I had not. This fact was confirmed by Dave who admitted that when we had come on the buffalo the second time, he had been able to pick mine out of the herd, because he had seen blood running out of a hole through its *ear*! Apparently, I had just nicked him. Then as we did a verbal postmortem on subsequent events. It turned out that my second shot had been taken at nearer 300 yards than the 200 I had estimated when I fired; so it was very possible that Dave had indeed seen the bullet strike the ground under the buffalo. I held out no real hope for the third shot and was slowly and reluctantly being reconciled to the fact that, apart from grazing it the first time, I probably had not hit him at all. In any event nothing could be done until morning.

Although Dave was pretty certain that the buffalo was virtually unscathed, still we could not take that chance without investigating. One always has to go after possibly wounded animals, but this time it was doubly true, because we were hunting on a ranch where there were herd boys, wandering about and tending cattle. If one of them were to stumble unexpectedly on a wounded buffalo — if indeed it was wounded — it could have fatal results. Although by now we were both reasonably sure that the wound was superficial, still we had to go back and have a look.

Record Peter's gazelle taken back in 1975.

We started right after breakfast — again in two cars. Our intention was to return and search carefully for blood. If we found nothing, we would then move on to hunt bush game. It did not take us long to find the spot. We left the others, and Dave and I started off on foot. I was carrying the same rifle as before, again loaded with a soft in the barrel

199

and solids in the magazine. Dave had a .300 magnum.

We nosed around for a few minutes until we came on the tracks of the herd that was now obviously long gone. Suddenly, Dave stopped and whispered, "There he is!" Somewhat desperately I searched the surrounding brush. For a moment I saw a black mass that might have been a buffalo, but it was only a stump. Then I heard Dave say, "Shoot!"

I replied stupidly, "I can't; I don't see him. Where is he?" I did not have long to wait for an answer.

The next thing I heard was Dave saying, "Here he comes!" Then a very angry buffalo charged from some thorn trees 25 or 30 yards away, with his nose up and grunting as he came.

At that point I experienced a strange psychological phenomenon. We have all heard that drowning people sometimes see their whole lives pass before their eyes as they are going down for the last time. Whether this is actually true or not I do not know, but I had something like this happen at the moment of the charge. My life did not pass before me. But I did vividly recall the many times since my first safari when I had told people that you simply *must not* be charged by a buffalo at close quarters. Someone is apt to get seriously hurt or killed — even if you succeed in killing the buffalo in the process. I remembered having said this many times, and now at the first instant of his charge I recall thinking, "Well, now we'll see if you were right when you said that it is almost impossible to stop a charging buffalo quickly enough." Strangely enough, I felt no fear, even though I knew only too well that within a second or two one of us might be killed.

You can never tell in advance just how you will react in a moment of extreme danger. On another day, like Francis Macomber in Hemingway's story, I might have broken and run in a blind panic. But that day I did not. I stood my ground next to Dave and prepared for whatever might happen.

What happened was that the professional fired. Trying for a brain shot, Dave's light bullet smacked somewhere into the buffalo's head. While it did not stop the bull, the bullet did stagger him. This momentarily broke his stride, and gave me the moment I needed to get my shot off, and I fired into his chest. My expanding soft nosed

That same Kenya safari yielded a record gerenuk a well.

bullet did terrible damage, taking the charge right out of him. The buffalo lurched sideways, obviously disoriented. Then Dave fired again, this time into the shoulder, probably breaking it. He went down, and I shot twice more as he tried to rise. As quickly as it had started, the crisis was over. All this had taken no more than two or three seconds, but in retrospect I can even now picture it as if in slow motion, like one of those action scenes in the movies. Incidentally, we learned later that on hearing the fusillade, our companions, who were not far away, beat a hasty retreat into their car, not knowing what was going on, but preparing for the worst.

The rest is anticlimactic. All the mysteries of the previous day were cleared up by a postmortem examination of the buffalo. As it turned out, I was pretty well vindicated, because I had done almost everything right. My first shot had indeed struck him right where I had aimed. If the bullet had been a solid, it would have penetrated the chest cavity, and everything would have been over in a few moments.

However, as it turned out, after going through his ear, the soft-nosed bullet hit the point of his shoulder at an angle and was deflected back under his hide. This caused a bloody, but harmless flesh wound. Yet it was this which had enabled Dave to recognize him the second time — and, incidentally, the next morning too. My second shot, fired at 300 yards, had hit just as I thought it had, but because of my error in range the bullet had gone low in the animal's brisket, narrowly missing his heart and passing out harmlessly on the underside of his body. It must have struck the ground some distance beyond, throwing up the dust Dave had seen and which at that range had seemed to be right under the buffalo. This caused him to think I had missed. Again it was a harmless wound.

Ironically, the one shot I thought had missed was actually the one that had done the job. Again, because of the greater than estimated range, I had not led the running animal sufficiently and hit him too far back. This gut shot would ultimately have been fatal, but in the meantime the poor beast would have lingered on in agony, perhaps for as many as four or five days. So it was good for all concerned that we found him when we did. I was also relieved to discover that my only real mistake — aside from almost deafening Dave — had been in badly misjudging the range on the second and third shots. Incidentally, he was a pretty fair bull.

I cannot close this account without praising the Lord for how everything worked out. In the first place it could only have been by His direction that we found the buffalo at all the next day. There was no blood, and the herd's tracks were all over the place, so we had no idea we were anywhere near him. Dave had no intention of pressing this for very long, because he was sure the buffalo had suffered nothing more than a superficial flesh wound. If our aimless wandering had taken us a 100 yards either to the right or left, we would not have seen him at all. In that case the least that could have happened would have been a painful and lingering death for the poor buffalo. More likely, however, was the chilling prospect that in the process he would have killed some unsuspecting boy, tending cattle.

Secondly, we can be thankful that once having found him, neither one of us was injured or killed. Dave's sharp eyes had spotted the

This is the Cape buffalo that almost got us.

buffalo's legs under the thorn tree behind which it was standing. If Dave had not seen him then, the bull would have caught us completely by surprise, and it would have been quite problematical whether we could have stopped him in time. As it was, it was a near thing and much too close for my comfort.

In retrospect this experience only confirms my observations on the danger of the buffalo. Do not underestimate this wild animal. Never let yourself be lulled into a false sense of security by its apparently ox-like behavior when undisturbed. Nor should you assume that just because nine times out of 10 a wounded bull will flee, it will necessarily do so the tenth time. Remember that there is a limit beyond which *mbogo* cannot be pushed. If that limit is reached, and if it is still on its feet, he will turn and fight. And when he has made up its mind to fight, nothing will change it but death — either his own or yours. Always be ready to kill cleanly and quickly in the event of trouble. If you don't, you will be killed. When it is finally provoked to a charge, there is no more dangerous creature on earth than the African Cape buffalo — a noble and very brave animal of the African bush.

Chapter 25

Clare and the Swimming Pool On Safari

After each of my safaris I wondered whether I would return again. Then after my solo trip in 1993, I was certain of it. Being alone on safari had convinced me that this type of hunting was not all that great. It is so much better to be with others, so I believed that the "end of the game" had come for me. Then when Phyllis died in 1995 after a long and heroic struggle, the wisdom of this decision seemed to be confirmed.

However, it was not too long before I fell in love again and married a wonderful woman whom Phyllis and I had known for 25 years. Needless to say, I then wanted to go on at least a short safari to introduce her to the wonders of the African bush. But there was one problem: Clare is a Southern Belle from North Carolina. As such she was totally unfamiliar and uncomfortable with the idea of sleeping in a tent with wild beasts roaming through camp at night, using the somewhat primitive facilities often associated with safaris, and, above all, with no electricity for her hair dryer. The last thought was the one that *really* threatened her sense of well being. We had a problem, but perhaps a compromise could be worked out.

Ralph and Gunlog Millet, former safari companions, heard of a wonderful three-week tour in southern Africa, and they convinced us to join them. I never thought the day would come when I would be a *tourist* in Africa, but one has to make some concessions in life. However, Clare had to make one too: if I were to be persuaded to go on a tour, she at least had to agree to a short big game hunting safari tacked on to the end of it. With fear and trepidation, she agreed. Consequently, in 1997 I booked an eight-day hunt with Garry Kelly Safaris, the company with which Phyllis and I hunted 14 years earlier in Zululand and the Great Karroo.

Sighting in the rifle at the start of the safari.

The tour was interesting. Apart from seeing the usual sights in South Africa, we visited Victoria Falls, going briefly into Zambia and then spending a day in Botswana, where we traveled through Chobe National Park, an area I knew from hunting on the Chobe River. All in all, it was not bad, but I was constantly anticipating getting into the hunting area of the Northern Transvaal, something I knew Clare was dreading.

Still hunting in 1997. My old greater kudu from the Transvaal taken in 1997.

Time did not erase car trouble. But in later year there was mechanized help available on the South African game ranchers. This one required a tractor to be brought in.

The author and Clare with his Cape hartebeest.

A very good greater kudu in the Chobe River area.

The tour ended and our friends headed for home. Clare and I stayed on and visited some old acquaintances, after which Garry picked us up at our hotel back in Johannesburg and drove two hours to our camp up north. As in 1983 this would be ranch hunting, but I knew perfectly well that, while it would not be like the old times, the hunting itself would be challenging, and there would be some very good heads available. With the hunt being so short, I was really after only one trophy: a superior Southern greater kudu. I took a nice East African kudu in 1971 and a fair southern one in 1990 in Zambia, but I wanted something much better. I had been assured that there were some very good ones where we would be hunting. However, one problem would be that it was early April, the beginning of the southern hemisphere's autumn, and the leaves would still be on the trees, making it very difficult even finding the animals. It would be challenging hunting, but the big problem would be to get Clare settled into a lifestyle that would not outrage her southern sensibilities. However, when we rode through the gates of the ranch known as *Bonwa Phala*, our jaws dropped with astonishment. The "wilds" of the African bush turned out to consist of large, beautifully thatched huts, complete with electricity, flush toilets and hot and cold showers with unlimited water. Clare's eyes danced with joy and relief. That was not all: This ranch was designed to take non-hunters as well, so there was a handsome main building with a modern kitchen, dining room and a well-stocked bar. Then we discovered a *swimming pool* just beyond our hut. At this I could tell that we really would be roughing it. To top things off, there was even a young steenbok wandering about camp. It had been abandoned as a fawn and raised on the ranch. Consequently, it had no fear of humans, but it was beginning to show unmistakable signs of reverting to the wild. It was getting to be that time of year when a young steenbok's fancy turns to romance. Needless to say the week we spent there was painless, in fact luxurious, and as I have begun to push into the upper decades, it was really not all that bad. In fact, it was rather nice.

The hunting was really uneventful and without any particular incidents. Initially, I shot a typical southern impala for camp meat. Clare, who never before even heard a gun go off, wept when she saw it stretched out dead. I thought to myself that this was going to be a difficult hunting trip. Since it was only average in size, I only took the hide for a rug. Then as time and shooting progressed, Clare not only stopped weeping as animals dropped, but even decided she would like an impala head for our second home, a condominium in Connecticut, which up to that time had been absolutely virginal as far as hunting trophies were concerned. So it became necessary to shoot a second one, and she was even photographed with me, her hand resting on the dead impala. Things had certainly changed in a few short days. To sum it all up, I did indeed get my very nice kudu and in addition, a very good impala, and an excellent red hartebeest. This last was a new species for me.

The upshot of all this has been that what was *definitely* to be my last African hunt, may not be after all. Plans are beginning to percolate for another safari. My middle son, Randy, who was in at the start of all this in 1971, wants me to take him, along with his son, John, and my daughter's son, Ben, in 1999. How can I possibly resist such a request!

Chapter 26

Ave Atque Vale

As the reader may gather, I have returned quite a few times to "drink of the waters of Africa." Starting in 1971 with my two sons and continuing for almost 30 years, I have gone over seven times and hope for one more trip. Twice I hunted in Tanzania, and once in Kenya, where it all started about 100 years ago. I have also hunted in Botswana, in Zambia, and twice in South Africa. During the twilight of the old classic safari I became intoxicated with Africa — when the veldt was not yet overrun with cattle and there was still plenty of game. I remember those 31 days in 1971, when my sons and I were in Tanzania, that we saw 64 lions. Granted, they were of all types: males, females, and cubs, but they were lions, nonetheless. Now it is not unusual to go through a whole safari without seeing any of the great cats. Today so much of Africa is simply being overrun by cattle. And with their inoculation against the once fatal bite of the tsetse fly, along with the destruction of so much of the woodlands for firewood, the impact on wild life is devastating. As cattle move in, game moves out. The problem is that now there is no place for it to go. I am grateful to have had a glimpse of Africa as it once was — at least as it was at the very close of the golden years. But now the end appears to be in sight, and I do not want to be there when it happens.

There are so many memories: the cheerful *"hodi"* before dawn, rolling out into the icy early morning, swatting the tsetse flies as the sun got warmer, worrying and fretting while struggling to winch the hunting car out of dry river beds, hearing the plaintive call of the wood dove, and, perhaps above all, sitting in the smoke of the campfire under the African sky with a cold martini in hand while listening to the sounds of the night — the hyenas' "whooping" and perhaps even a distant lion's roar far out on the veldt. I loved sitting around while Dave

Camp at Oloitokitok (1975). Mount Kilimanjaro can be seen in the distance.

An ox-bow lagoon near the Tana River in Kenya. This was once great elephant hunting country. Alas, no more.

The author and his Coke's hartebeest.

A close relative to the above, taken on a different safari, the Lichtenstein's hartebeest.

Some were confused.

Ave atque vale to the old Africa.

Ommanney. We swapped improbable and probably embroidered tales from years past, arguing over the circumstances of some of my former efforts at hunting African game with him or at my futile attempts to roust him out of his tent as the day threatened to leave us behind. My efforts were futile, because he always insisted that game does not move around during the heat of the day, and humans with any intelligence shouldn't.

It is always good to get back into the bush and to smell Africa again. The classic safaris of my father, Ernest Hemingway, and Robert Ruark — even my own in 1971 and 1975 — are now only memories, yet life on the African veldt still has the power to intoxicate. It was for this reason, much more than for shooting, that I returned so often. Even now, if I were 20 years younger and had all the money needed for a 60 or 90-day safari that would necessitate traveling to several countries, I would still like to go. I would love to get what Dave calls a "hairy lion" — one with a circus mane. I would like to complete the "big five" with an elephant and a rhino, and I would jump at the chance to hunt the remainder of the spiral-horned antelopes: Mountain nyala, bongo, and giant eland. However, such hunting is only a pipe dream — at least for me. In a way I am not sorry, because over the past few years the horn of the hunter has sounded fainter and fainter for me. I will always treasure the memories of my hunting that started when I shot my first white tailed deer with my father in 1937. At that time I was only 10 years old, but the chase was on. Subsequently, there were two pack trips with him into the Canadian Rockies and many more hunts over the years at our camp in Nova Scotia. I have no regrets — except over those very few animals that I wounded and lost. However, down through the years I have shot so much that I am now satisfied with my experiences. I do expect to return once more in 1999 on a sentimental safari to South Africa with my son, Randy, and two grandsons, who will then be 15. These two youngsters will represent the fourth generation of African hunters in my family, and except for the "Cottar Clan" of professionals, I do not think many people can make such a claim. When I return, my own hunting objectives will be most limited — perhaps a Cape kudu if it is 50 inches or more, and maybe a black springbok. I would much rather watch others do the shooting. Apart from that if I ever do go back in later years, the game will have nothing to fear from me unless some elephant or lion drops dead from fright at hearing the click of my camera. I hope I have not quite drunk from the waters of Africa for the last time, but before long, as Harry Tennison says in his book, it will be the end of an affair when I sadly say, *Ave atque Vale* — Hail and Farewell.

Chapter 27

Kwa Heri, Na Jambo

The sun has set on the old Africa. Colonialism is over, and nationalism is on the move. Africa is emerging from its past and seeking integration into the world community. A possibly bloody tribal political struggle is still a threat in the south. But the rest of the continent is fighting another kind of battle, one for its very survival: an economic one, a struggle to gain and preserve arable land, as the population explodes and as the Sahara moves inexorably southward.

Earlier in the century when Africa was mentioned, the "Dark Continent" and a vision of the lion, the elephant, and the safari usually came to mind, but no more. Today the hard reality is a population expanding out of control, a struggling third-world economy, the results of the overthrow of *apartheid* in South Africa, intertribal strife, terrorist attacks, vast numbers of people perishing from almost annual droughts, and the specter of perhaps 100,000,000 people dying from AIDS during the next decade.

Almost forgotten are the last remnants of the rhino, a relic of the Stone Age almost hopelessly fighting to survive in the atomic age. The elephant is being driven toward extermination by avaricious men slaughtering it with automatic weapons, greedy for the gold they gain at the sacrifice of his ivory. And fainter and fainter grows the lion's roar.

Must we say good-bye to the old vision entirely? Is there no controlling the flood of humanity that threatens to drive the last traces of a glorious natural heritage into oblivion? Or is there still hope that in a new Africa there may yet be found a corner or two for the wild animals? There are a few years left, but then the wildlife will be gone, unless the emerging nations recognize what they are on the brink of losing forever. At the present time some of the new governments give

Wire snare carried by the hartebeest after pulling free from this "anchor."

Faru on the move. They too are making a comeback.

lip service to the preservation of the game, but when push comes to shove, when the wild animals are forced to compete with cattle and even human beings for land, the game always loses.

There are a few voices crying out to save at least a remnant of the vast herds that once covered the veldt in their endless search for food and water and for the predators that were never far behind. We can only hope that those who want to save the game — whether they are government people for economic reasons, conservation groups, or paradoxically the world hunting community — we can only hope that they will succeed. We can only hope, as inevitably we must say good-bye to the old Africa and greet the new, that something will remain. We hope that the veldt may never be completely emptied of its herds and that the African night may still echo to the roar of the lion under the Southern Cross.

THE END